Page

Patterns

Vol III

just plain
Simplicity

MW00380973

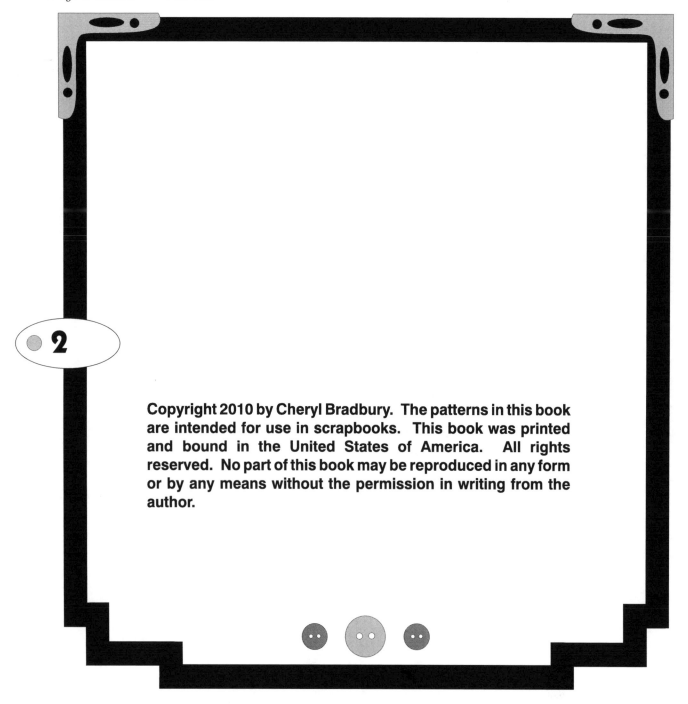

2

Copyright 2010 by Cheryl Bradbury. The patterns in this book are intended for use in scrapbooks. This book was printed and bound in the United States of America. All rights reserved. No part of this book may be reproduced in any form or by any means without the permission in writing from the author.

Introduction

As I've said before, creating my pages gives me such a wonderful feeling to know that I am leaving my family's legacy to generations yet to come. Creating and collecting all the various Patterns is almost an obsession for me and sharing them with you is a pleasure. I love to take a pattern and Re-Imagine it by flipping, turning and/or rotating it in order to make it look totally different. It may have the same basic design, but the Re-Imaging of it makes it a NEW and FRESH Pattern to use. For some of us, Re-Imagining a Pattern is difficult rendering us "Re-Imagining Challenged" and that is why I keep creating more patterns...with this said, I give you Vol III.

I am so delighted and proud to be able to share my newest book, "Page Patterns, Vol III" the latest prescription for "Layout Block". This book also has more than 600 unique and different patterns to help you map out your layouts. As with Vol I & II, they are "just plain Simplicity". The Patterns are clean, simple and easy to use because no-one elses photos are distracting you from envisioning your own photos into them. "Page Patterns" are so great that they work for the Beginner to the Advanced Scrapbooker.

"Page Patterns" can be turned, flipped, rotated and tweaked to fit your photos just way you need. Incorporated into these patterns are: plain and patterned paper uses and tons of embellishment ideas from brads, buttons, buckles, belts and staples to ribbons, ric-rac, tags, flowers and paperclips. Hopefully this latest set of over 600 "Page Patterns" will give you another recharge of motivation and inspiration in getting your layouts done and caught up.

At the front of the book, I've included an Embellishments Chart just in case you've never seen that particular embellishment. In the front and back of the book are Pattern Size Conversion Charts from the patterns, at their book size, for easy true-size conversion. Plenty of empty boxes to add in your own patterns for future layouts have also been included.

I hope that you will continue enjoying the fun of "Page Patterns Vol. III",

Just Plain Simplicity

Cheryl Bradbury

Have a Scrappin' 4 Memories Day

Embellishments Chart

	safety pin		photo corner
	turn buttons		envelope tie
	folder tab		frame hangers
	buckles		charms
	paper clip		hinge
	bread tag		staples
	bookplate		eyelet
	buttons		ric-rac
	tags		ribbons
	metal word plate		
	ribbon tie		swirl clip
	slide frame		flowers

4

Table of Contents

Doubles

2 Photos 9
3 Photos 13
4 Photos 17
5 Photos 23
6 Photos 29
7 Photos 35
8 Photos 41
9 Photos 47
10 Photos 51
11 Photos 55
12 Photos 59
13 Photos 63
14 Photos 67
15 Photos 71
16 Photos 75
17 Photos 79
18 & 19 Photos . . 83
20 & 21 Photos . . . 87
22 & 23 Photos . . . 91
24 & 25 Photos . . . 95
26 & 27 Photos . . . 99
28, 29 & 30 Photos . 103

Singles

1 Photo 111
2 Photos 117
3 Photos 122
4 Photos 129
5 Photos 135
6 Photos 141
7 Photos 145
8 & 9 Photos 149
10, 11, 12, 13, 14 & 15
    Photos 153

Embellishments Chart 4

Conversion Charts. 6 & 159

5

Patterns Size Conversion Charts

6

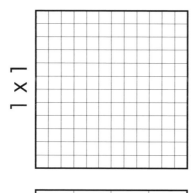 1 x 1

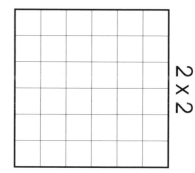 2 x 2

 3 x 3

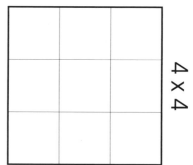 4 x 4

Use these conversion charts in helping to size your photos to fit the pattern your using. When fully sized, these charts and single Page Patterns are 12 x 12 and double Page Patterns are 12 x 24. Easily get correct measurements for your photos or mattings by matching your selected pattern against the conversion chart sizes.

Copy this page on to a Transparency for easier use with the Page Patterns.

Double Page Layout Patterns

7

PHOTO LAYOUT PATTERNS

D
D
D
D
D
D
D
D
D
D
D
D
D
D
D
D

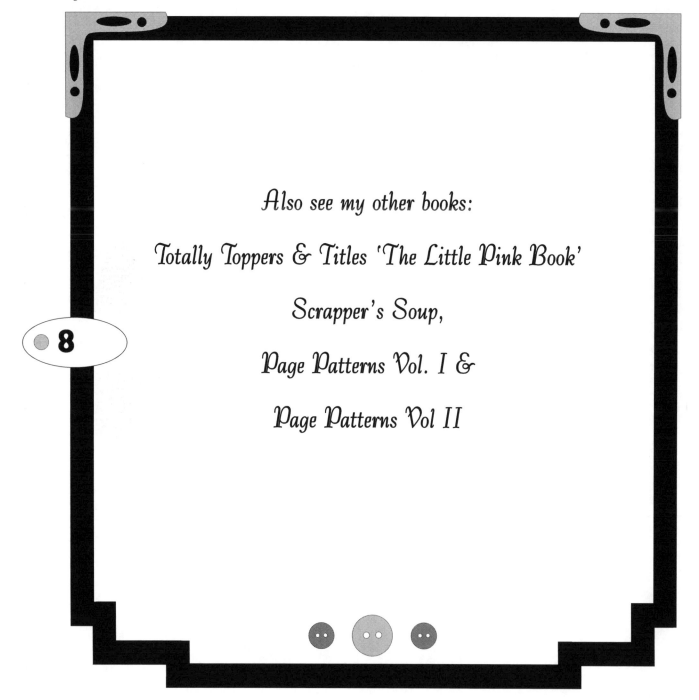

Also see my other books:

Totally Toppers & Titles 'The Little Pink Book'

Scrapper's Soup,

Page Patterns Vol. I &

Page Patterns Vol II

2

PHOTO LAYOUT PATTERNS

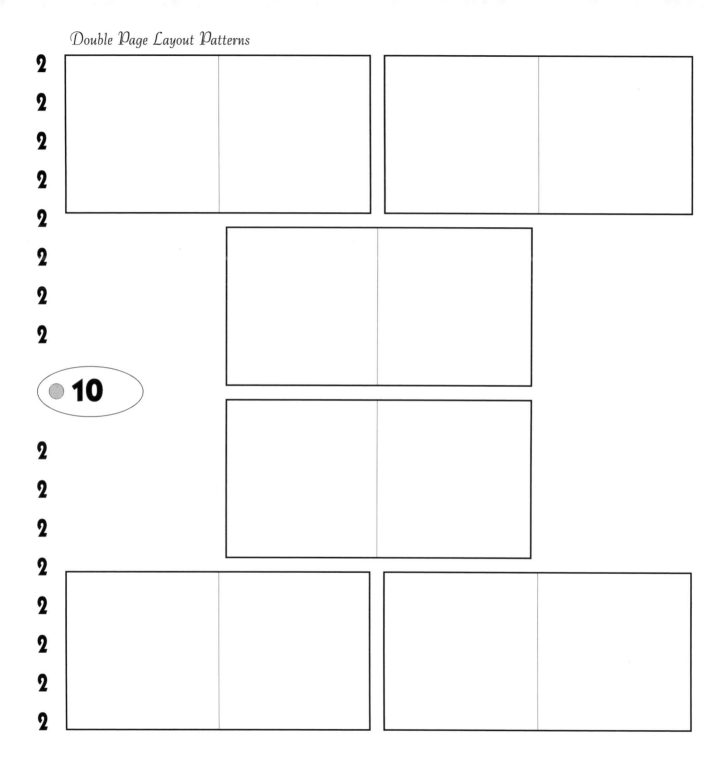

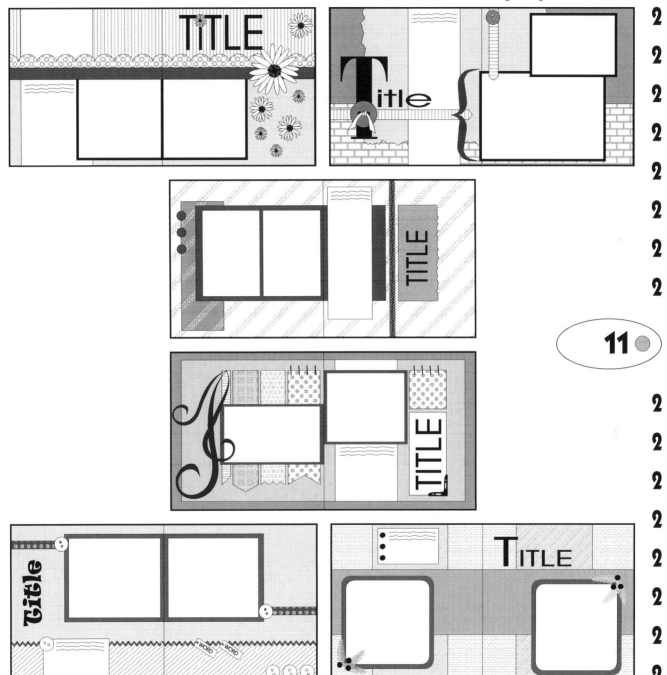

2 2 2 2 2 2 2 2 2

11

2 2 2 2 2 2 2 2

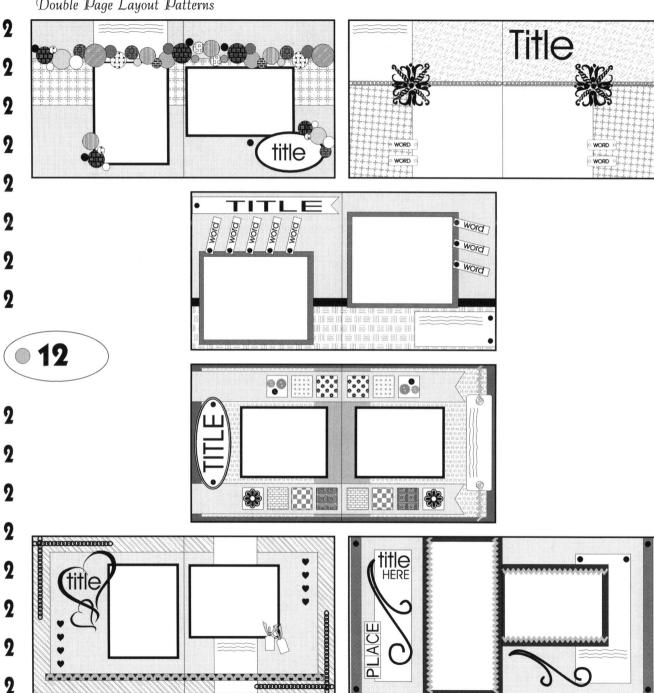

12

3

PHOTO LAYOUT PATTERNS

Double Page Layout Patterns

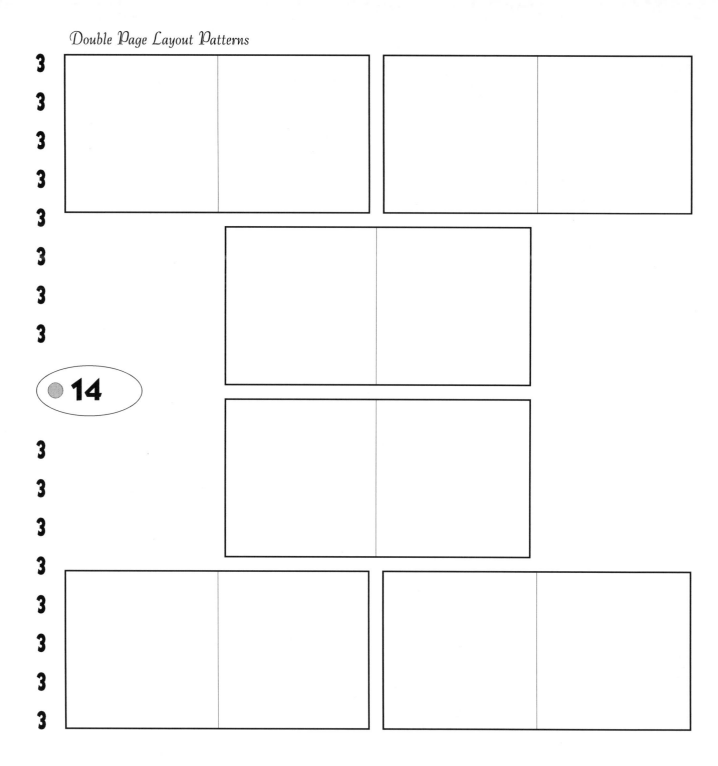

14

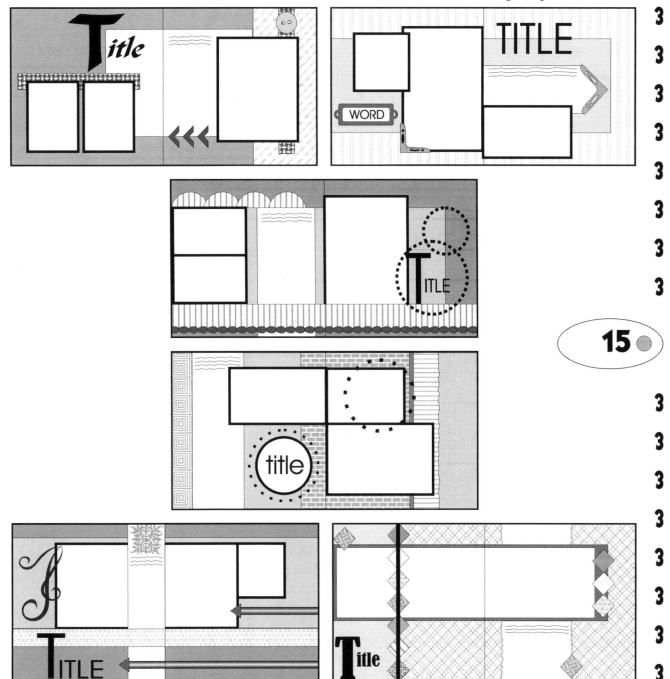

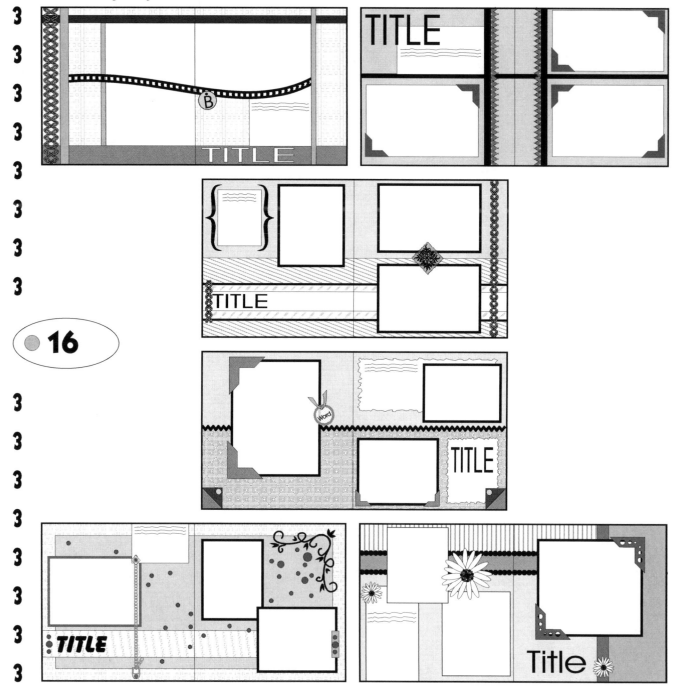

TITLE

TITLE

TITLE

TITLE

TITLE

16

TITLE

Title

4

PHOTO LAYOUT PATTERNS

4
4
4
4
4
4
4
4
4
4

4
4
4
4
4
4
4
4

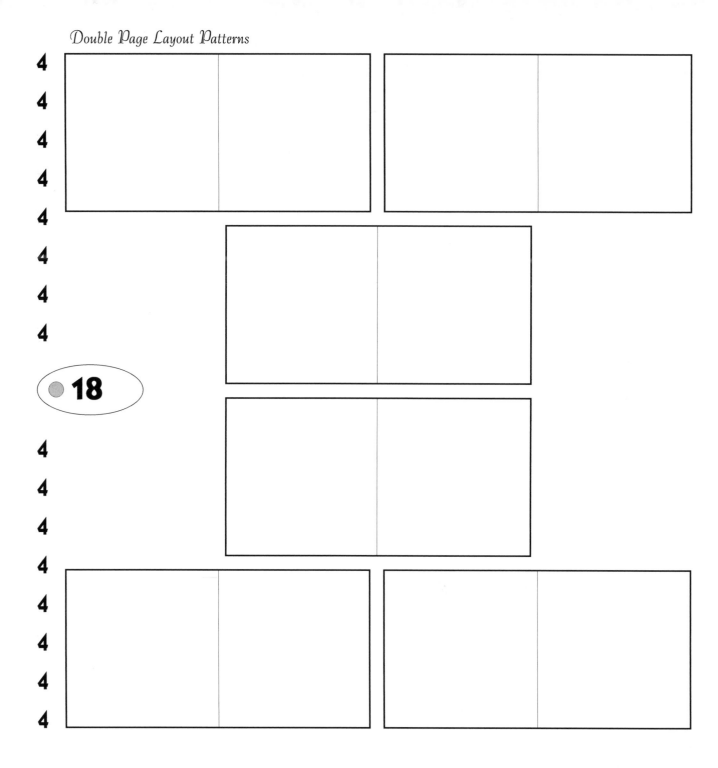

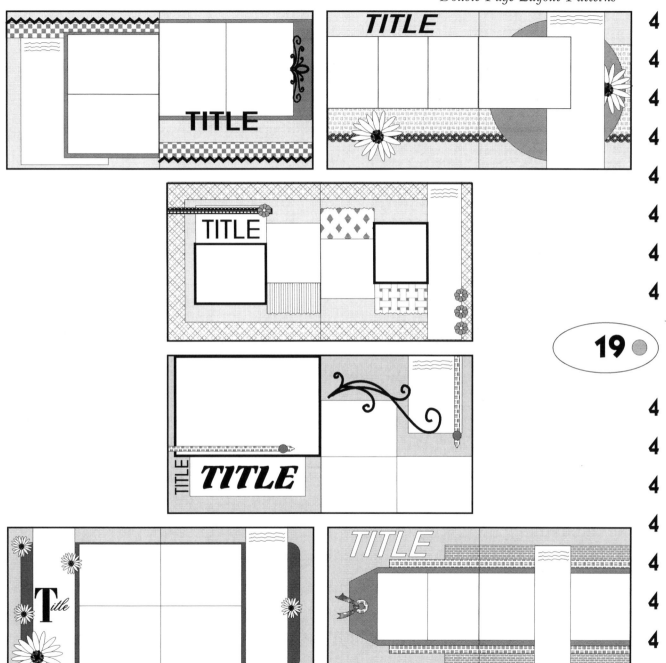

TITLE

TITLE

TITLE

TITLE

TITLE

Title

TITLE

19

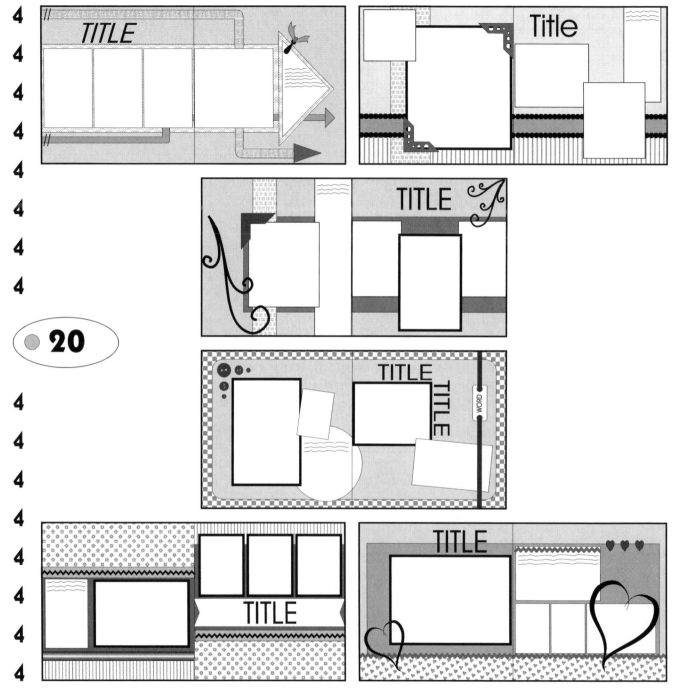

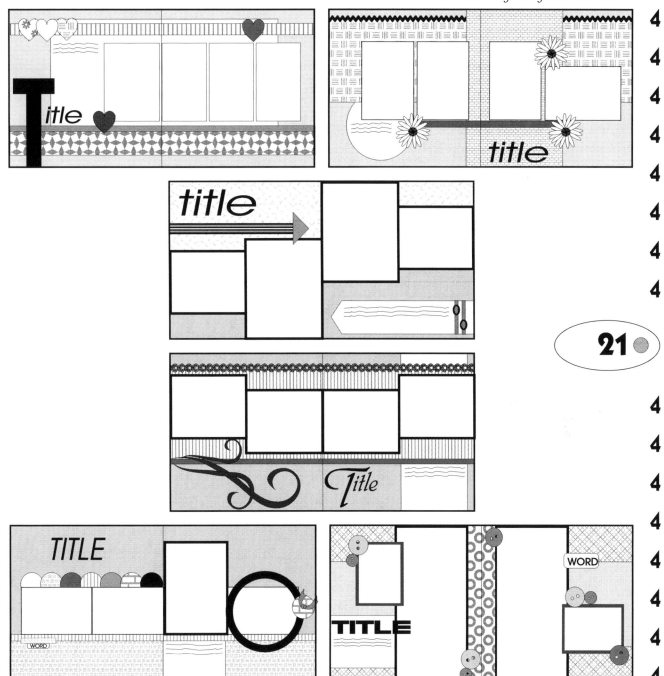

4
4
4
4
4
4
4
4
4

21

4
4
4
4
4
4
4
4
4

Double Page Layout Patterns

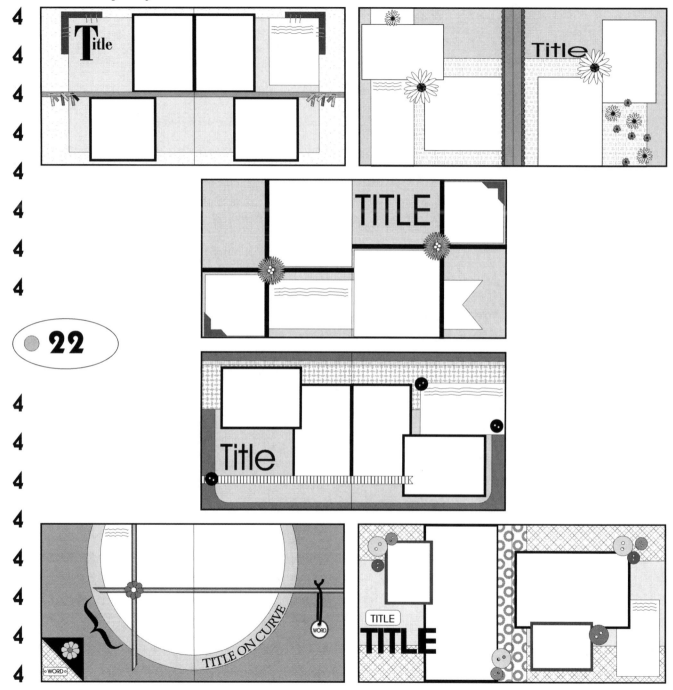

22

5

23 •

PHOTO LAYOUT PATTERNS

Double Page Layout Patterns

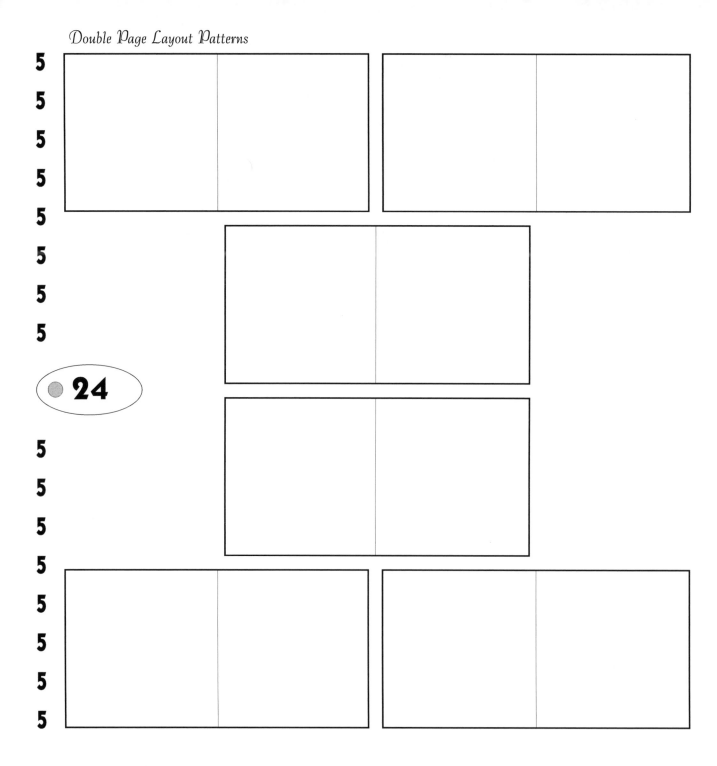

24

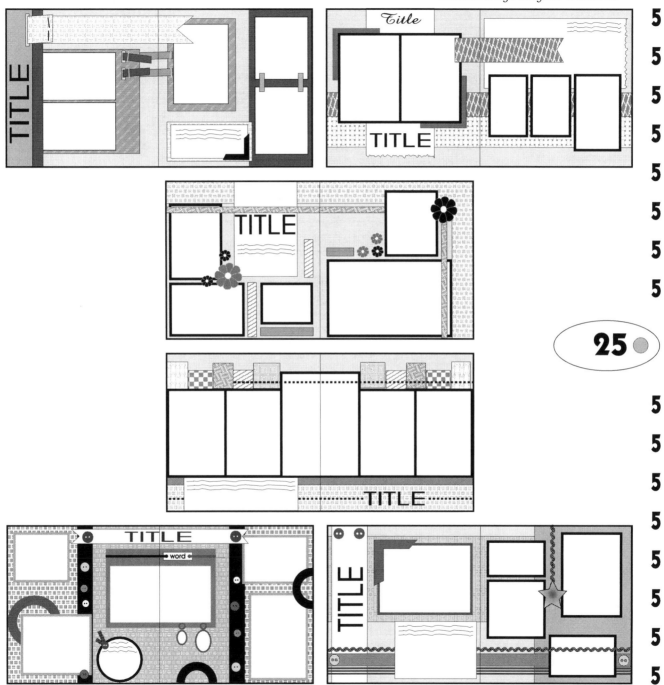

5
5
5
5
5
5
5
5

26

5
5
5
5
5
5
5
5

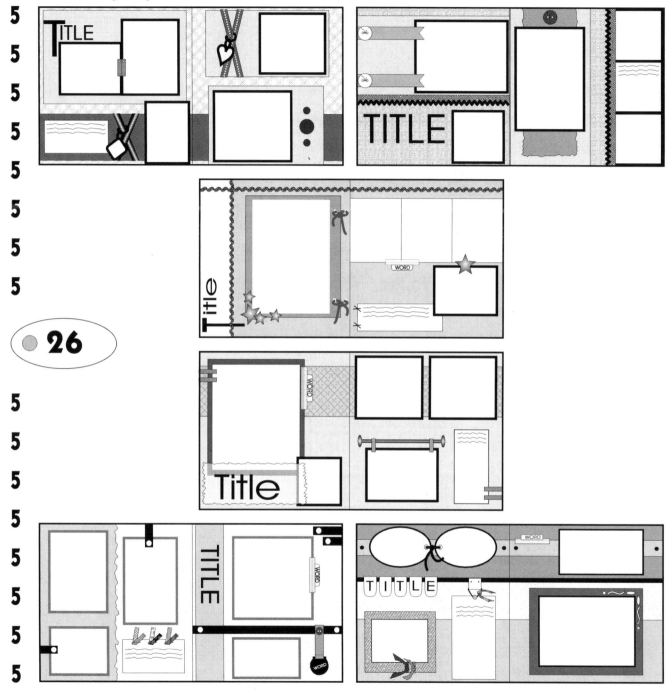

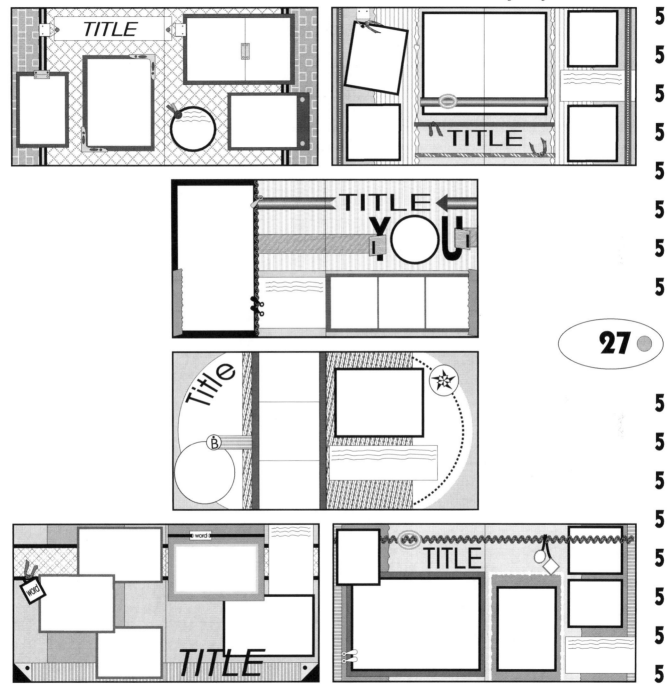

5 5 5 5 5 5 5 5 5

5 5 5 5 5 5 5 5 5

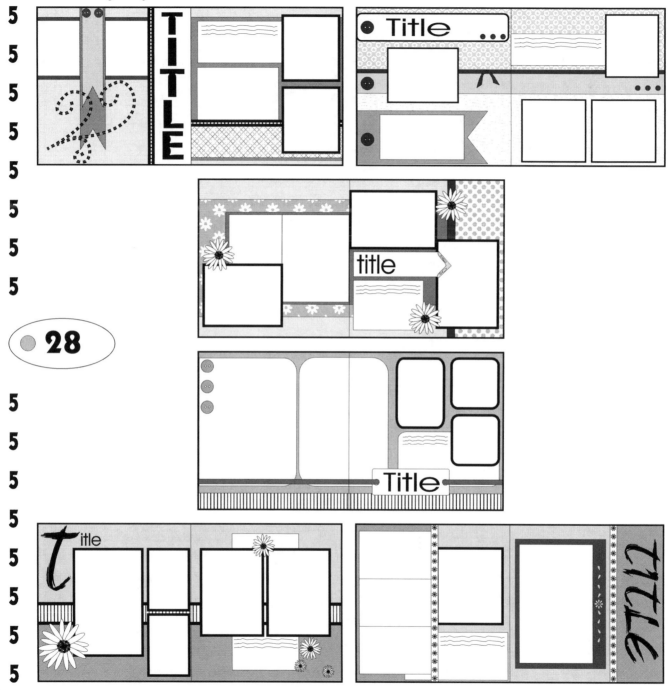

6

6

6

6

6

6

6

6

6

29

6

6

6

6

6

6

6

6

PHOTO LAYOUT PATTERNS

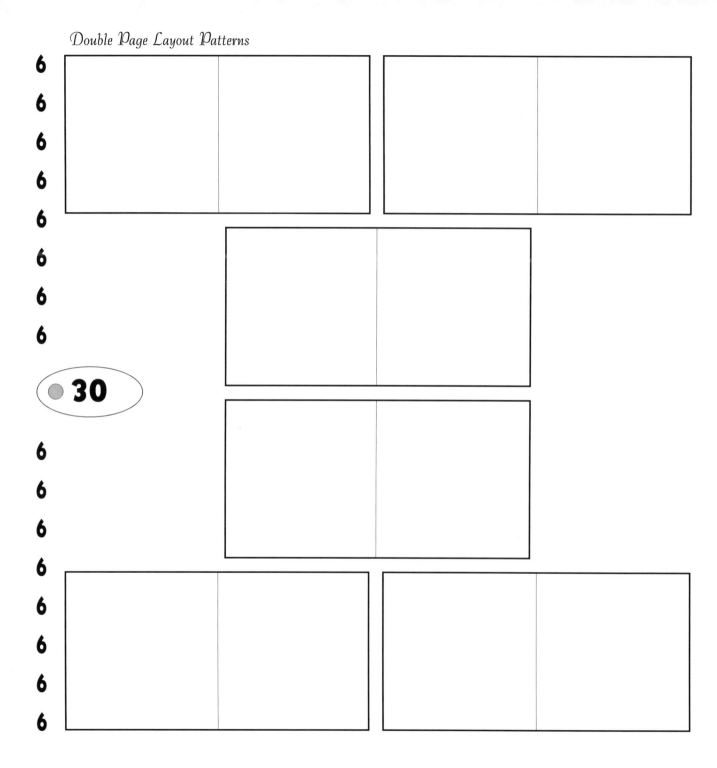

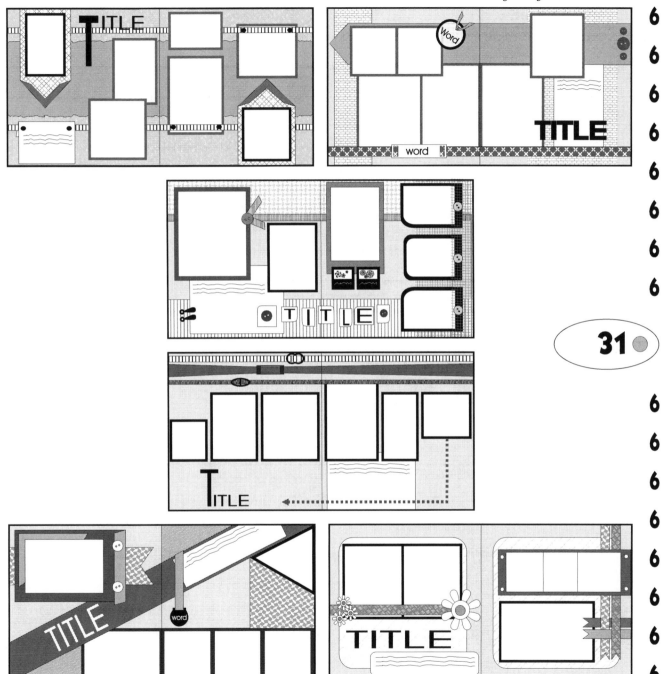

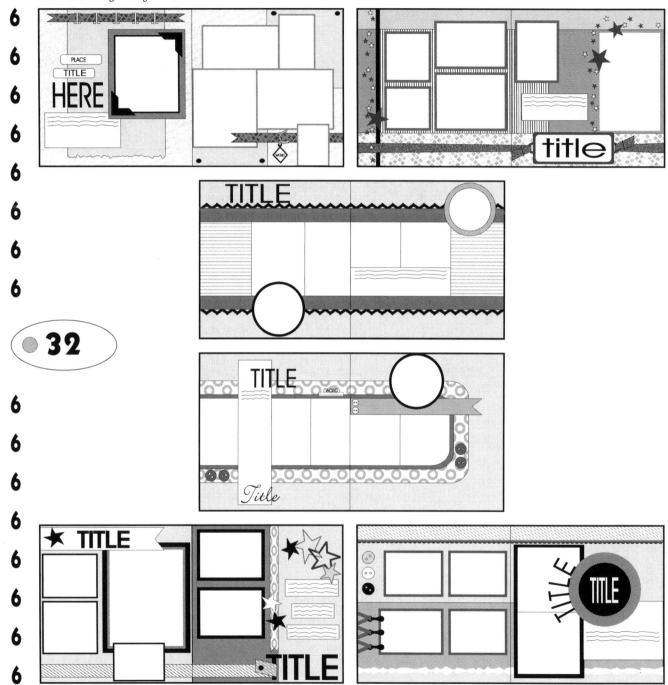

32

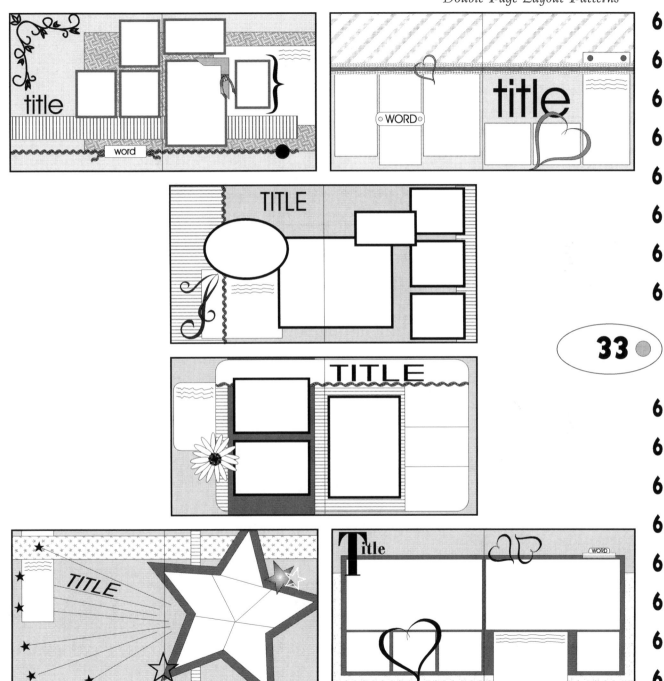

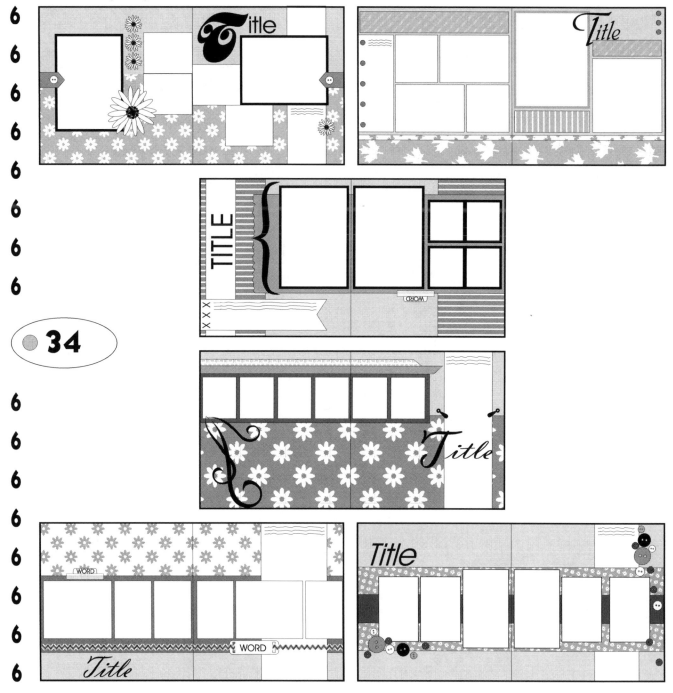

35

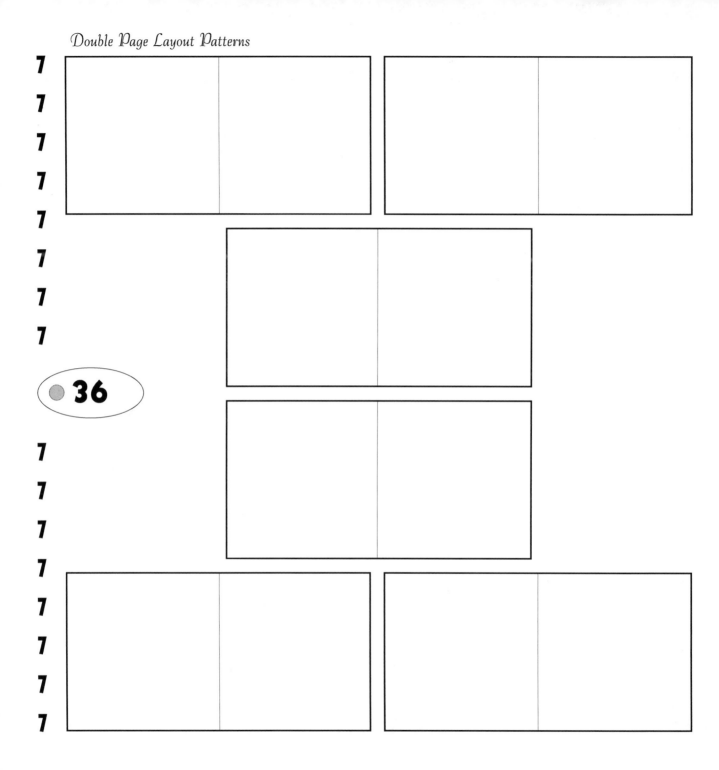

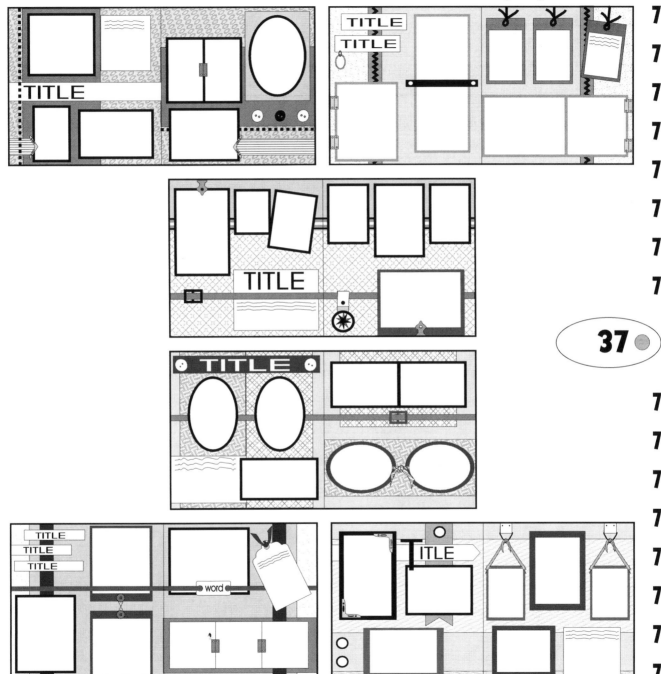

37

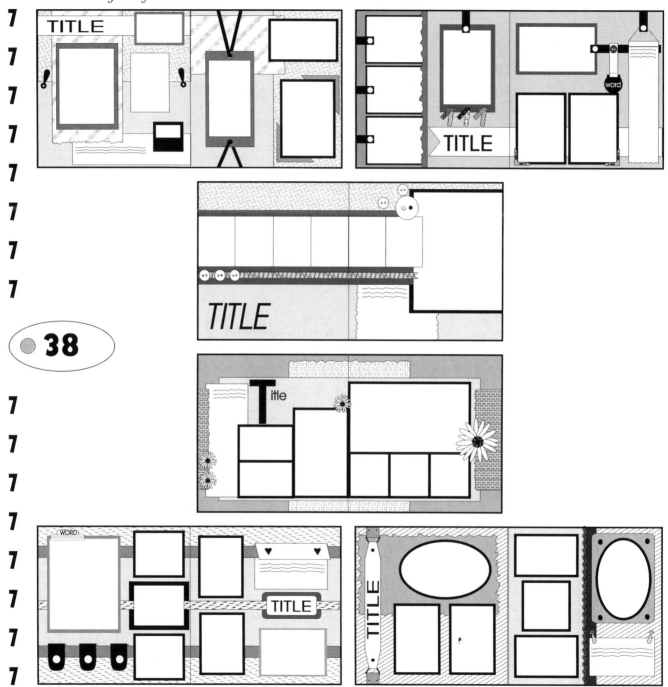

38

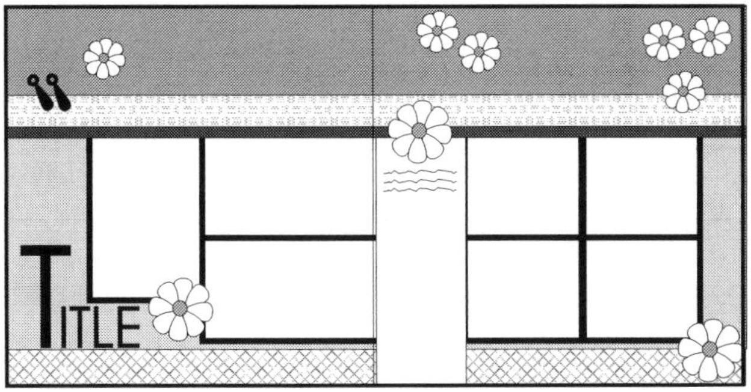
TITLE

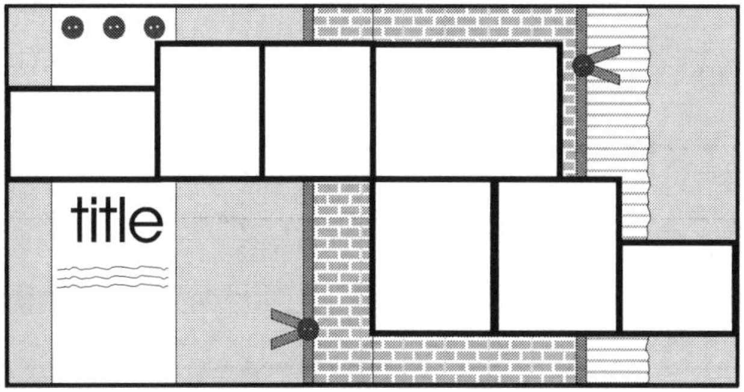
title

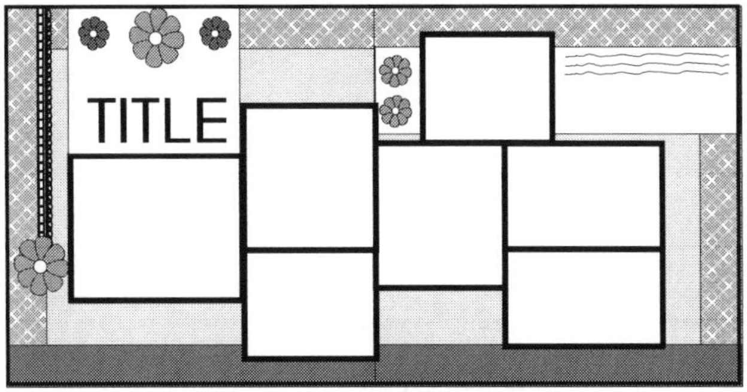
TITLE

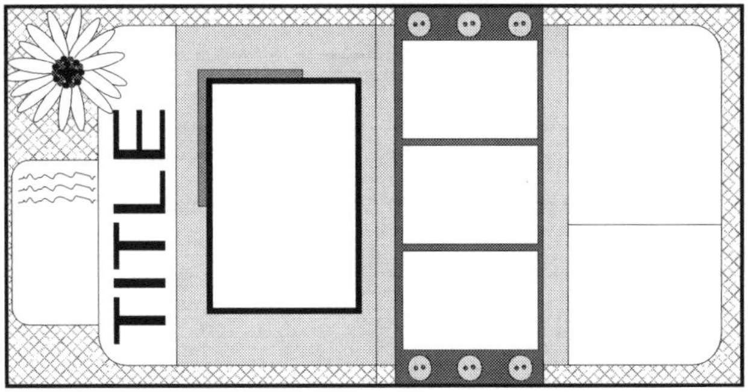
TITLE

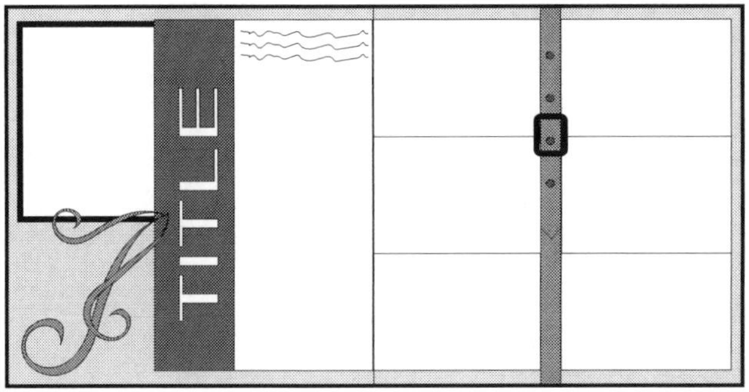
TITLE

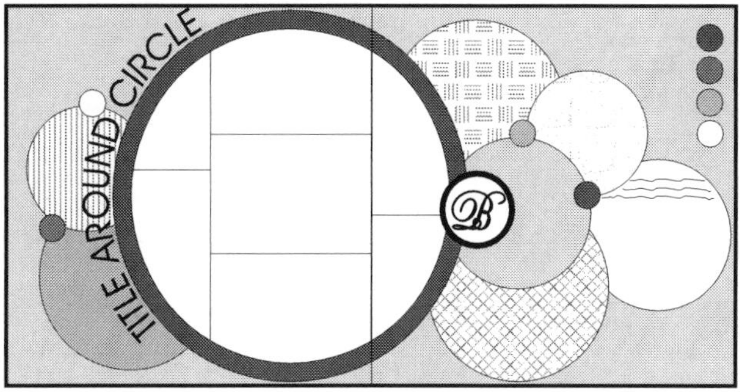
TITLE AROUND CIRCLE

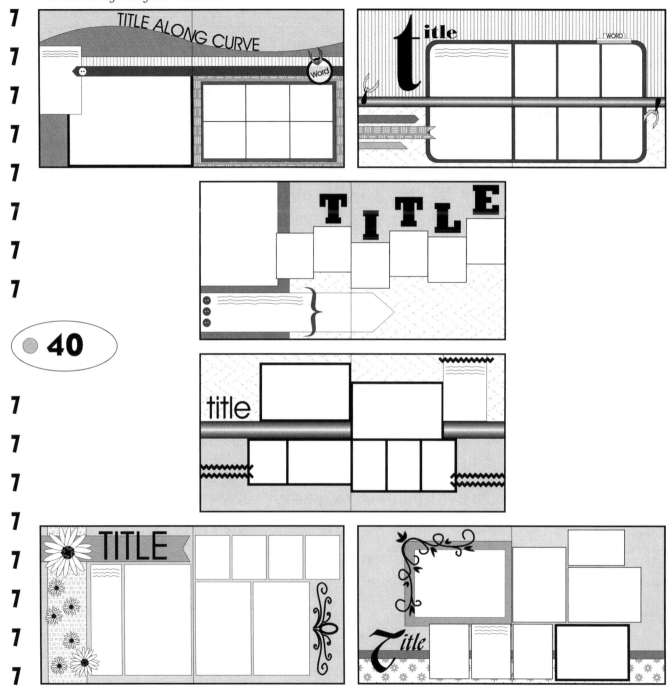

8

41

PHOTO LAYOUT PATTERNS

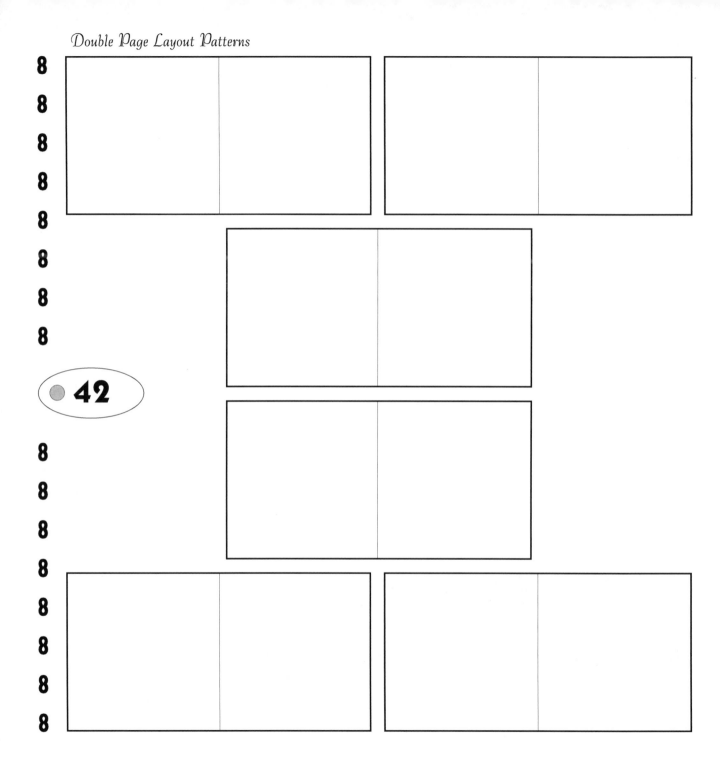

42

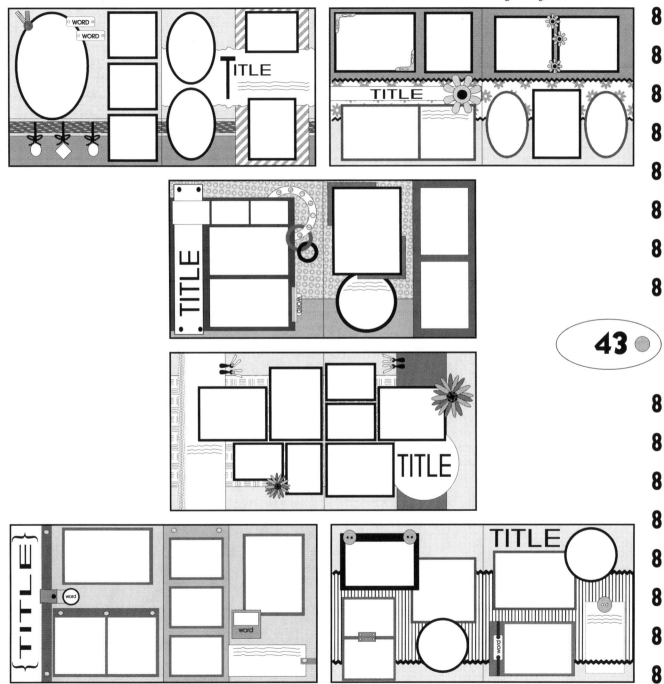

43

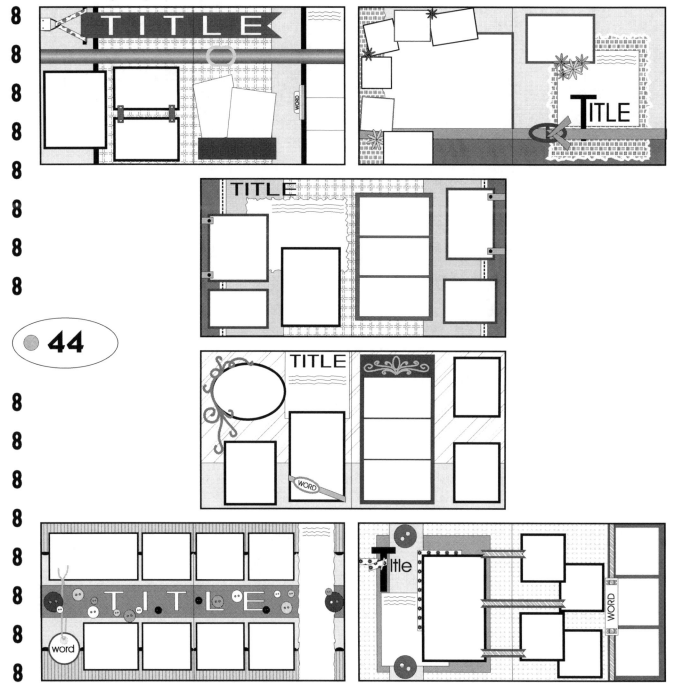

44

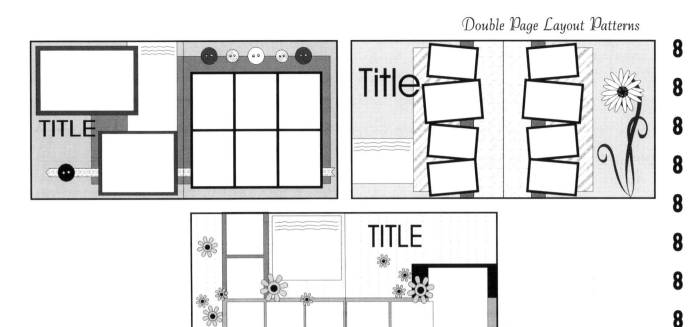

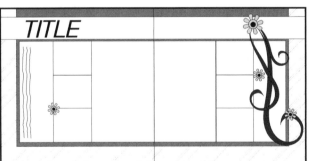

45

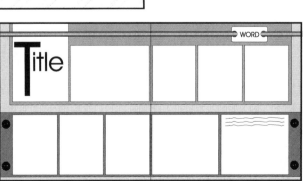

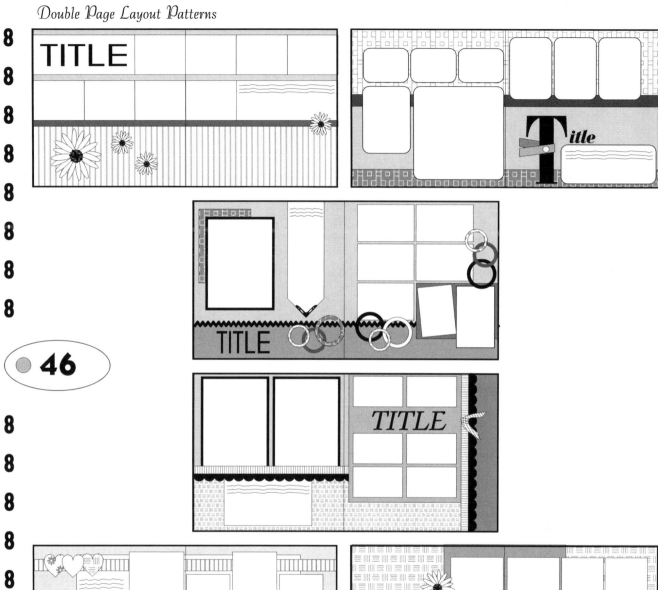

46

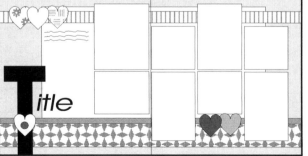

9
9
9
9
9
9
9
9

47

9
9
9
9
9
9
9
9

PHOTO LAYOUT PATTERNS

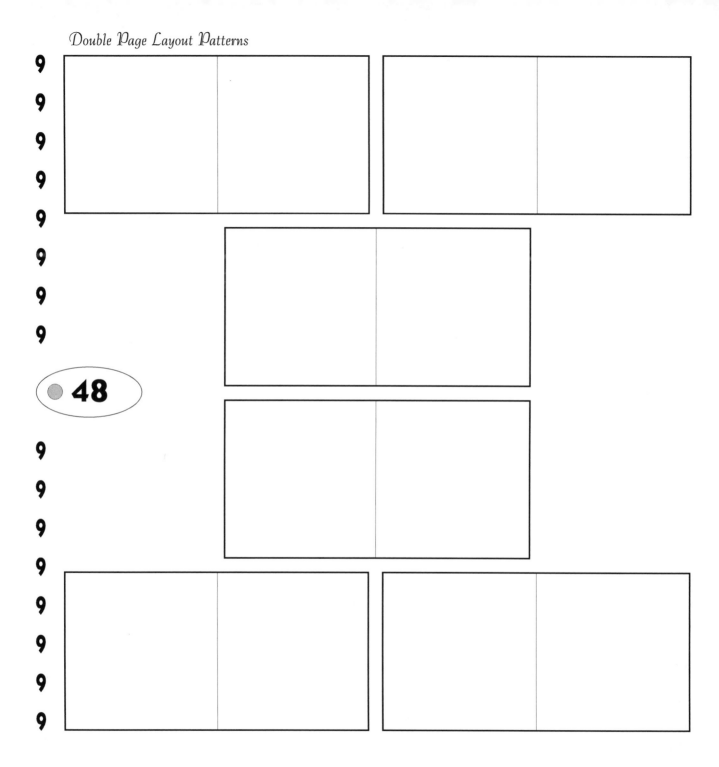

49

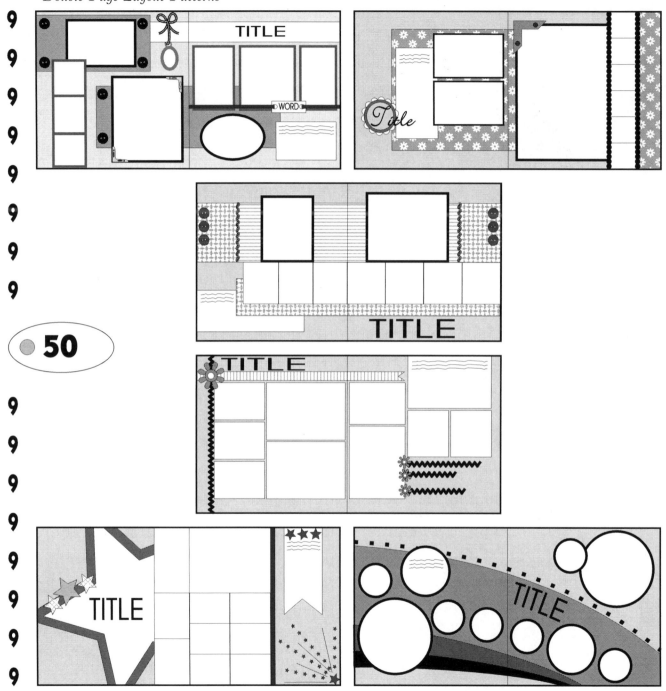

50

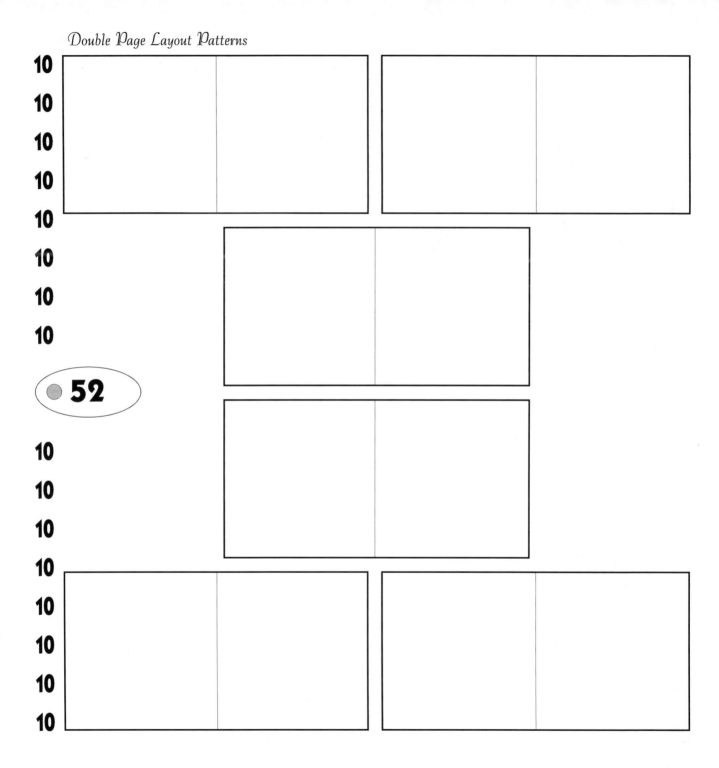

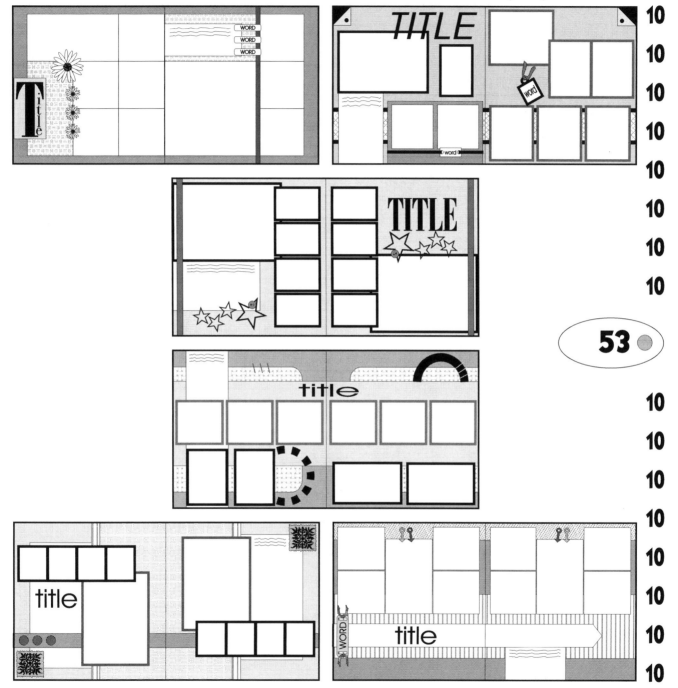

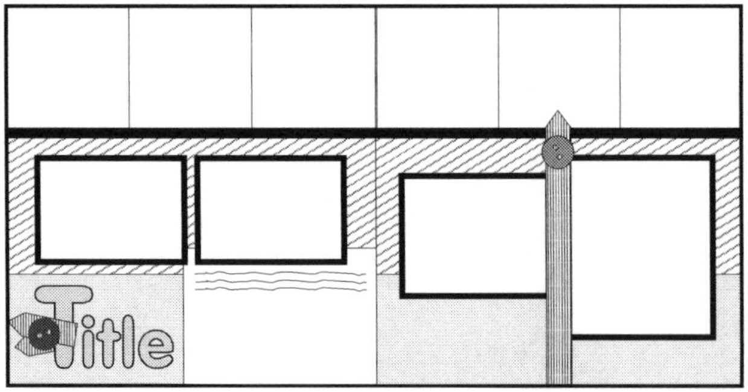

Double Page Layout Patterns

10
10
10
10
10

Title

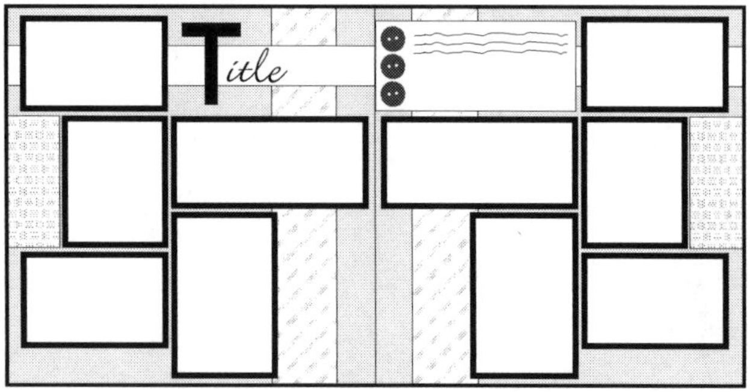

Title

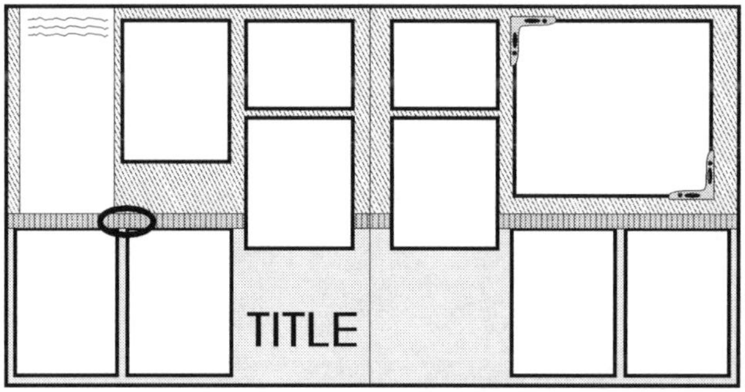

10
10
10

● **54**

TITLE

10
10
10

Title

10
10
10
10

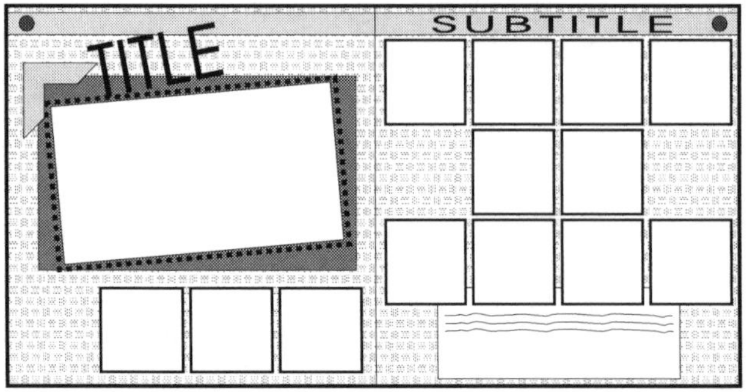

TITLE
SUBTITLE

Title

11

55

PHOTO LAYOUT PATTERNS

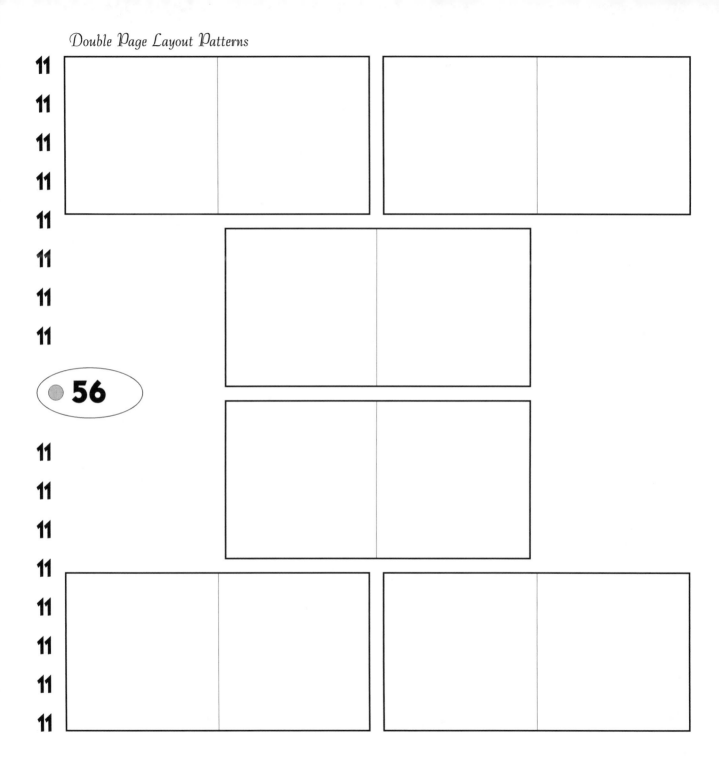

11
11
11
11
11
11
11
11

11
11
11
11
11
11
11

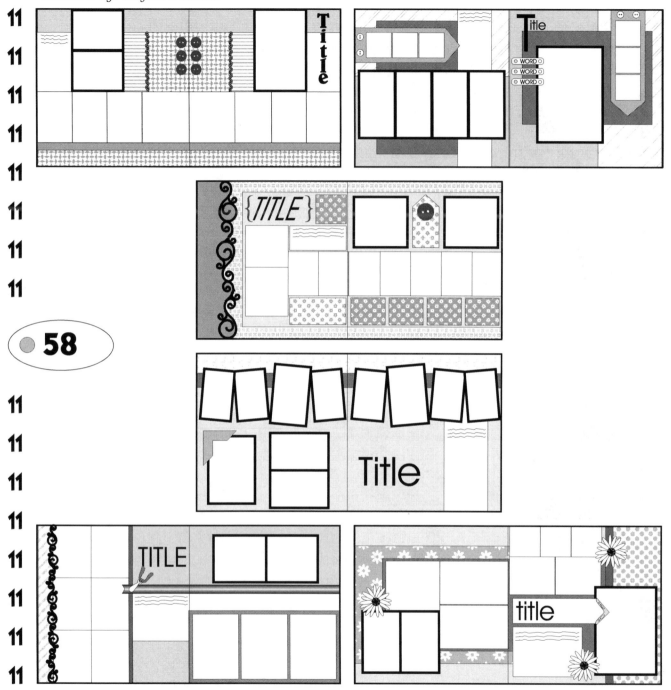

12

PHOTO LAYOUT PATTERNS

12
12
12
12
12
12
12
12

12
12
12
12
12
12
12
12

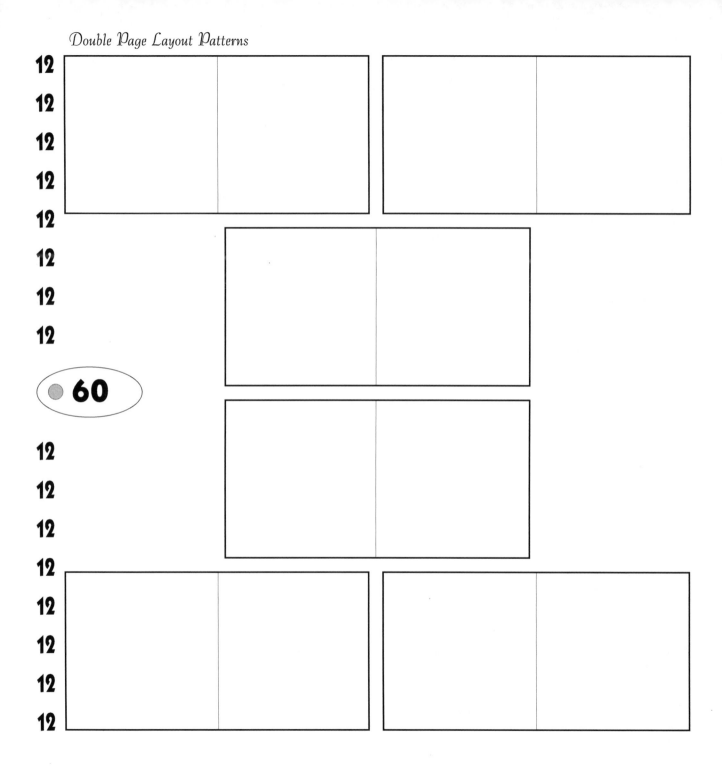

12
12
12
12
12
12
12
12

60

12
12
12
12
12
12
12
12

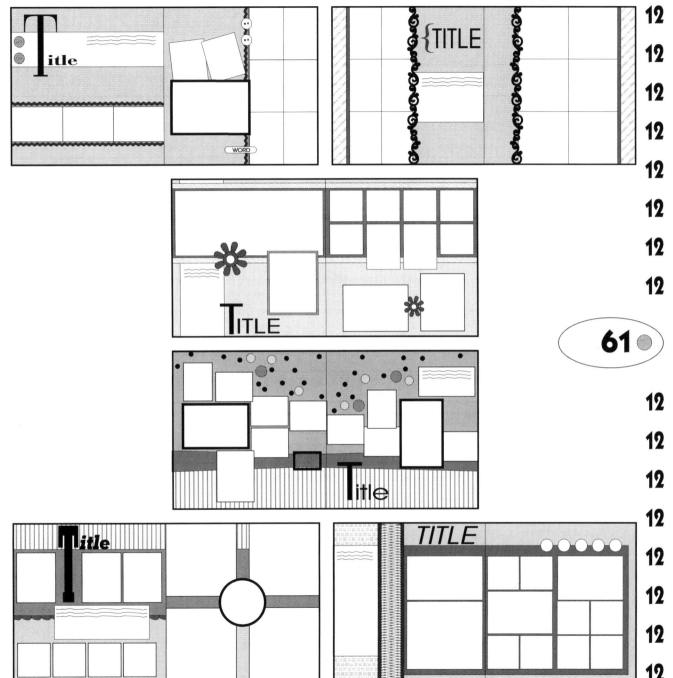

61

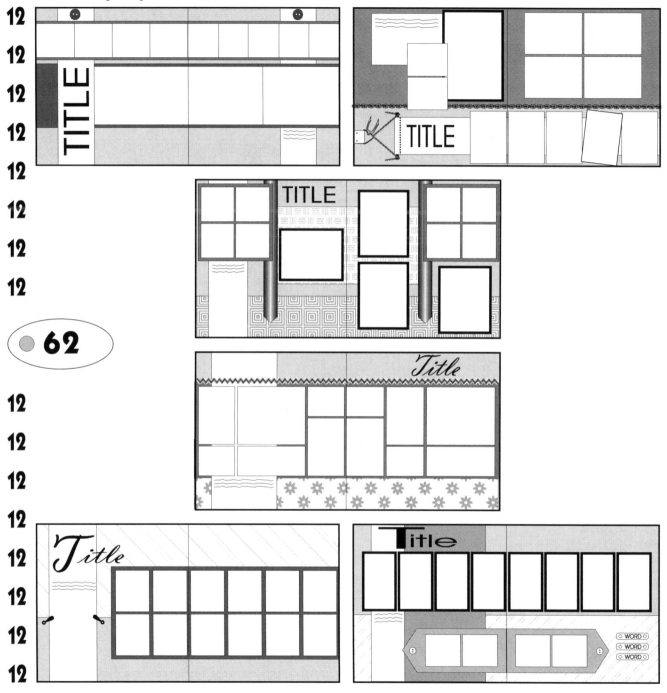

13

PHOTO LAYOUT PATTERNS

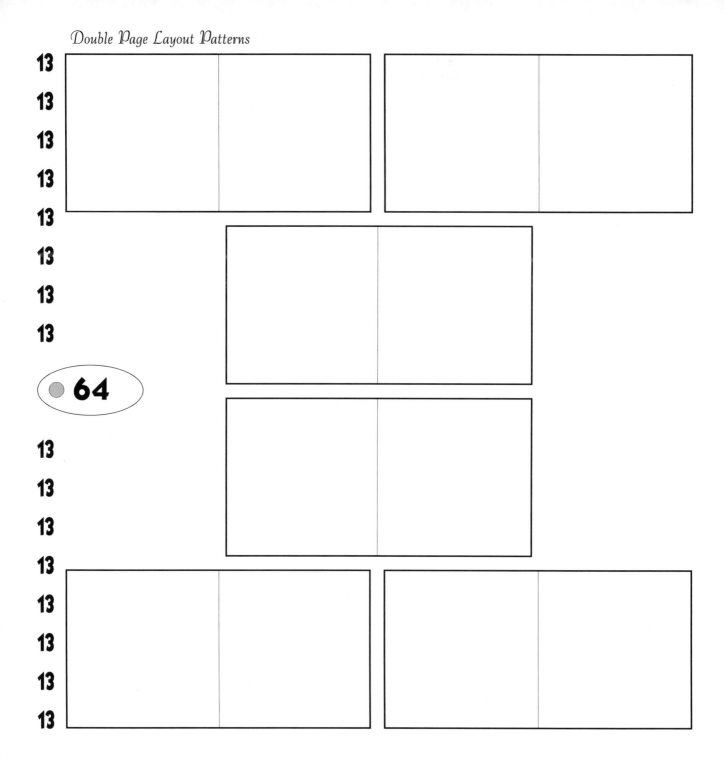

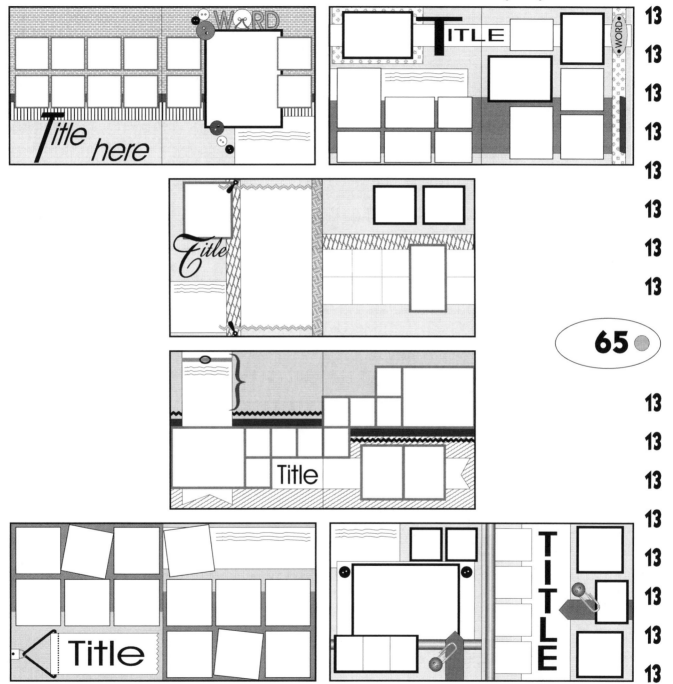

13 13 13 13 13 13 13 13 13 13 13 13 13 13 13 13

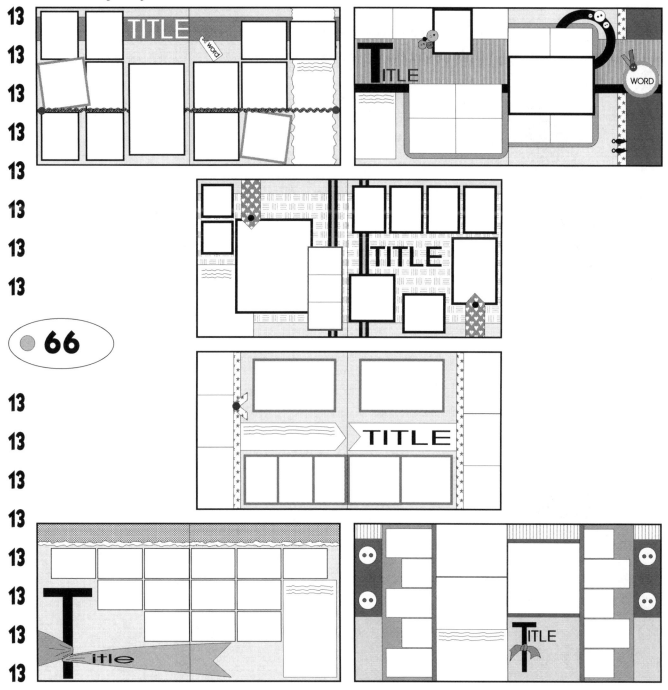

66

14
14
14
14
14
14
14
14

14
14
14
14
14
14
14
14
14

PHOTO LAYOUT PATTERNS

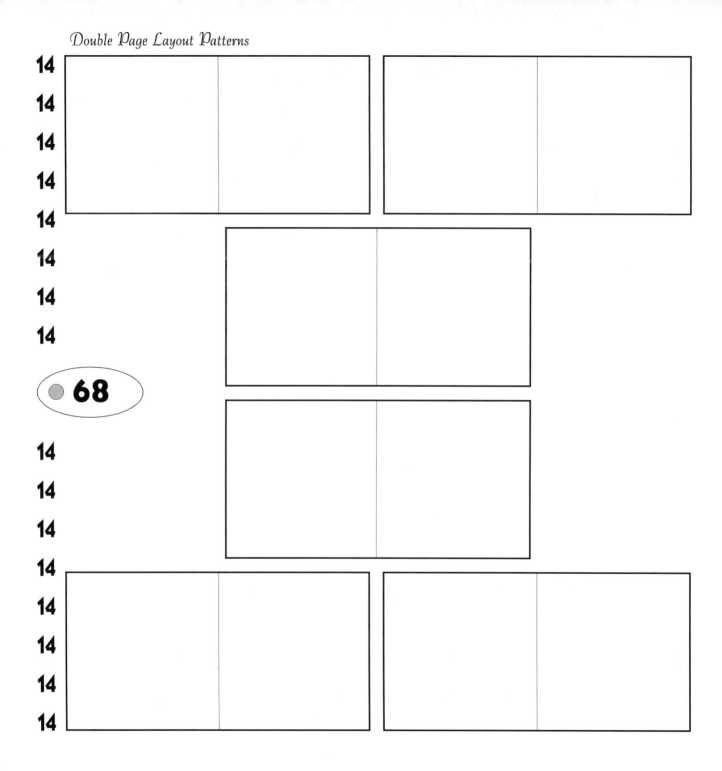

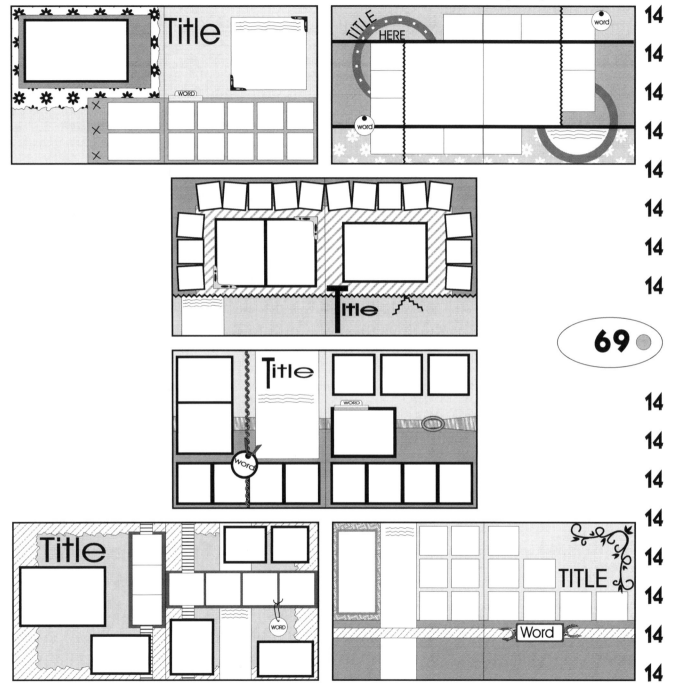

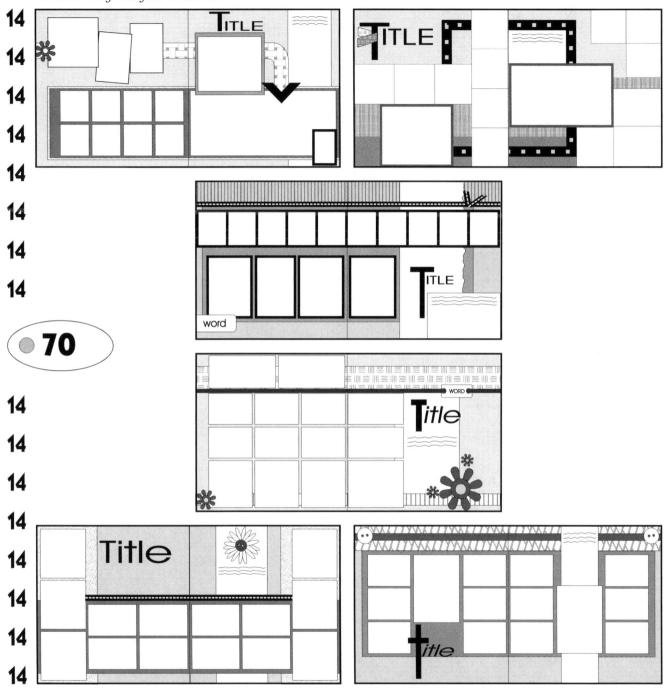

15

PHOTO LAYOUT PATTERNS

71

Double Page Layout Patterns

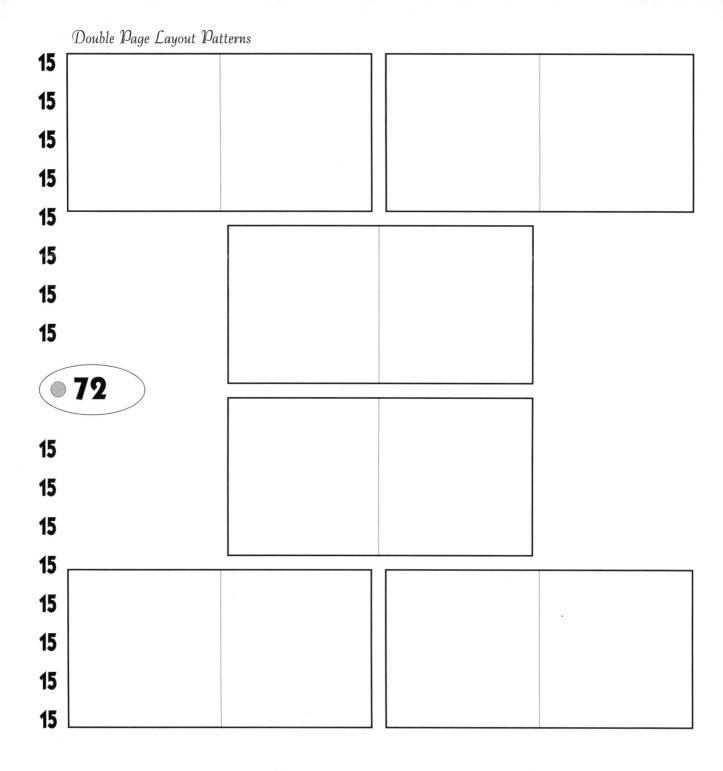

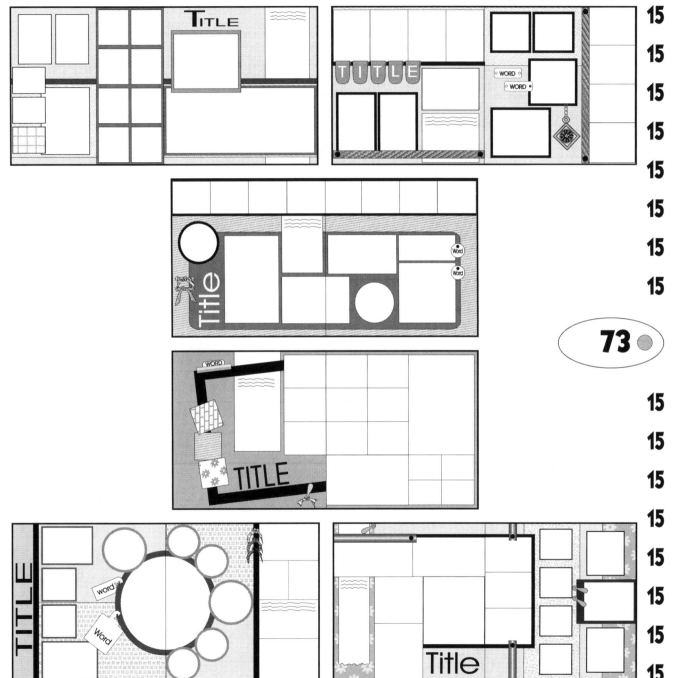

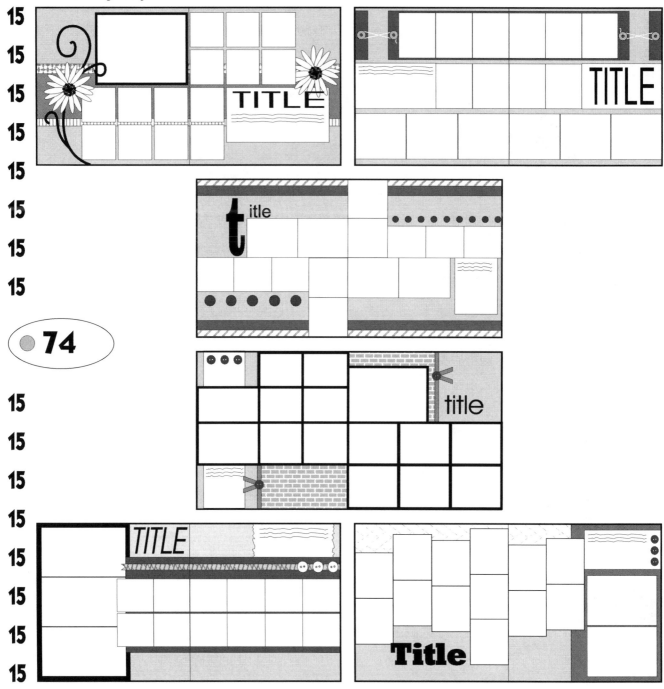

16
16
16
16
16
16
16
16

75

16
16
16
16
16
16
16
16

16

PHOTO LAYOUT PATTERNS

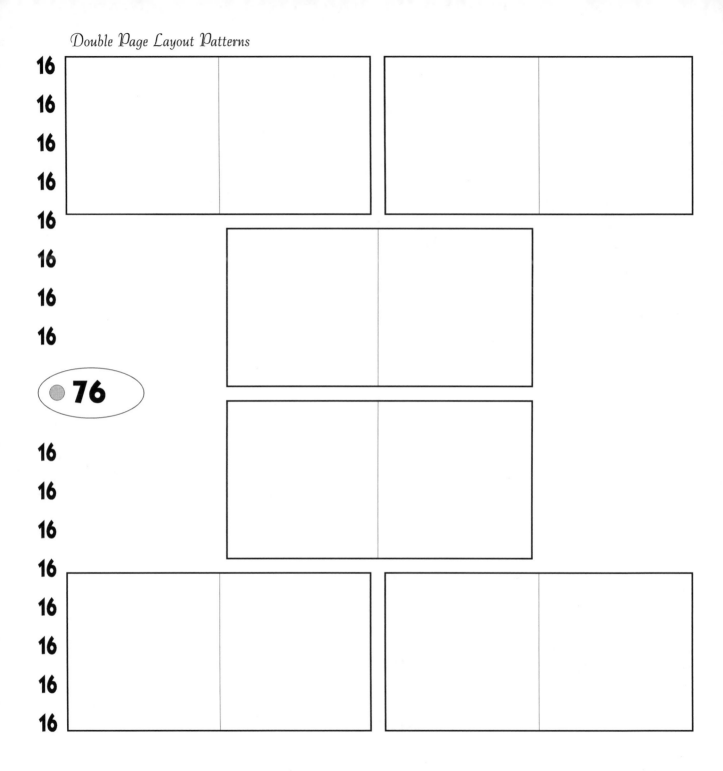

16
16
16
16
16
16
16
16

76

16
16
16
16
16
16
16
16

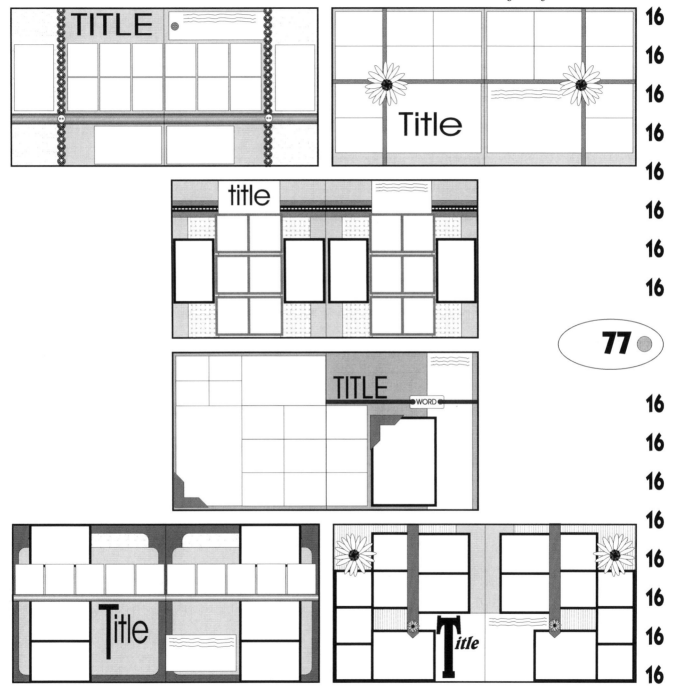

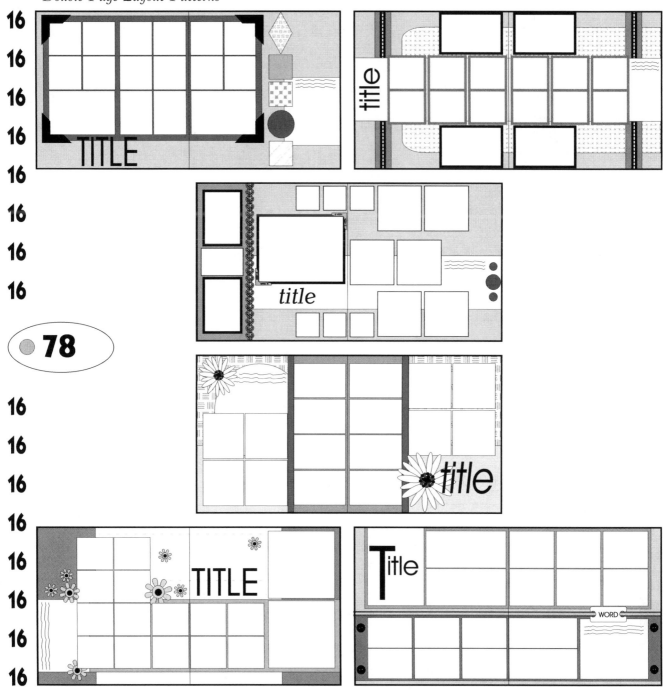

17

PHOTO LAYOUT PATTERNS

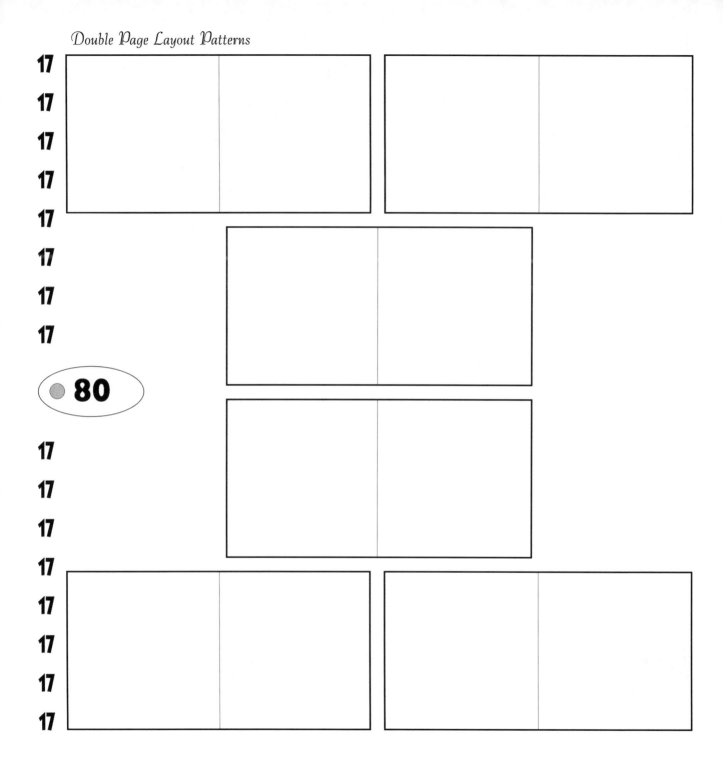

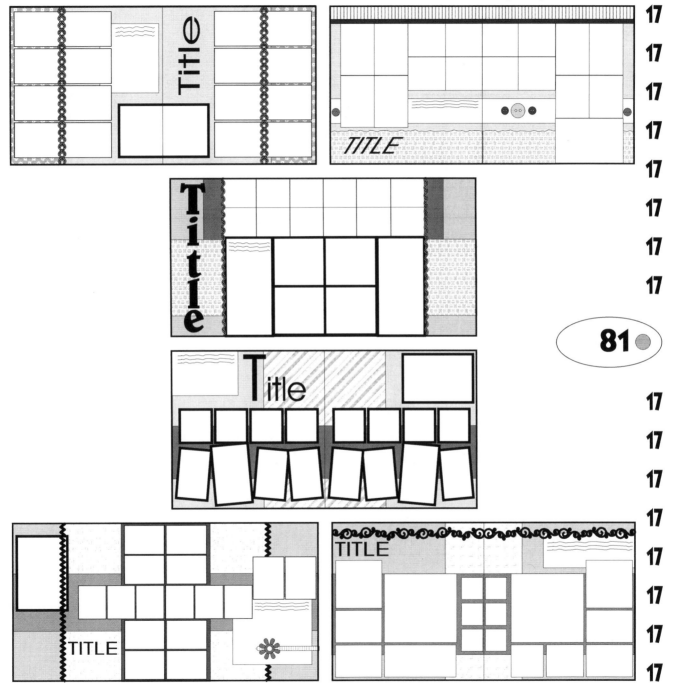

81

17

17

17

17

17

17

17

17

● **82**

17

17

17

17

17

17

17

Title

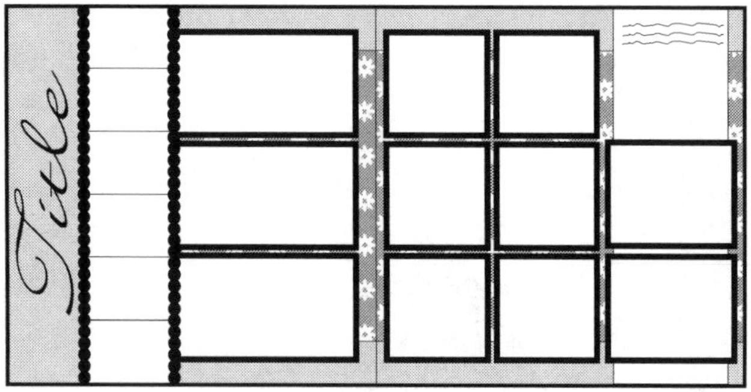

Title

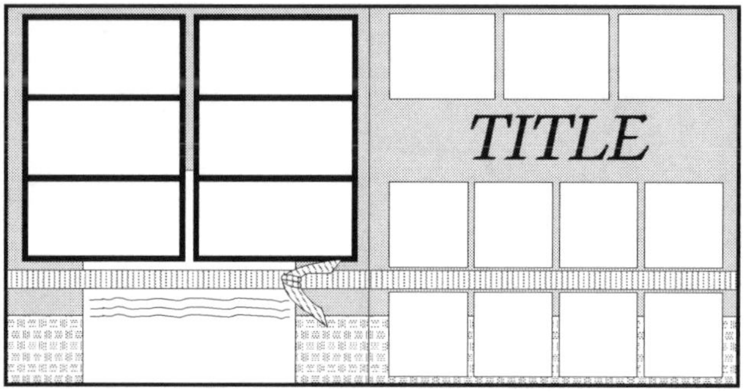

TITLE

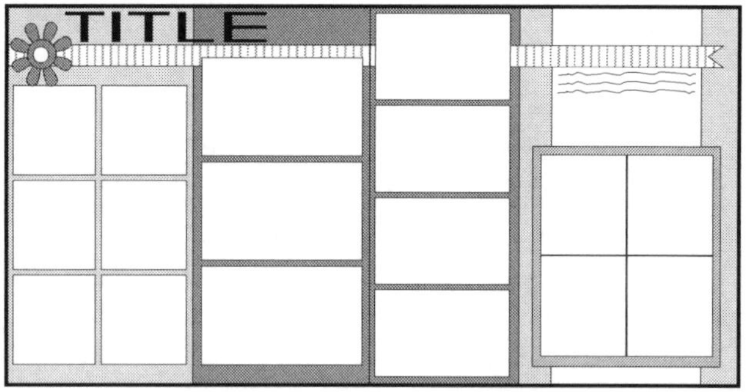

TITLE

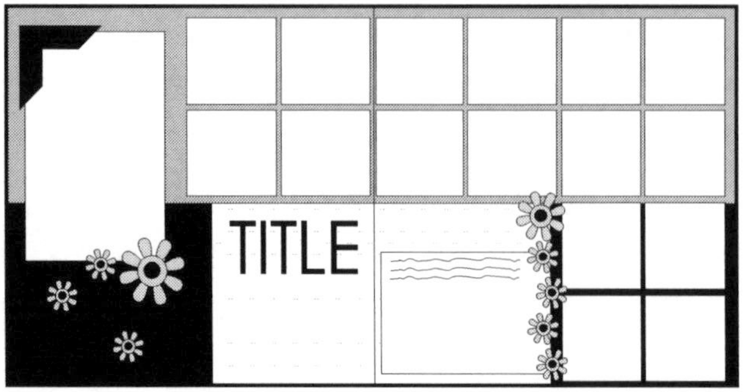

TITLE

WORD TITLE

18
19
18
19
18
19
18
19

83

18
19
18
19
18
19
18
19

18 & 19

PHOTO LAYOUT PATTERNS

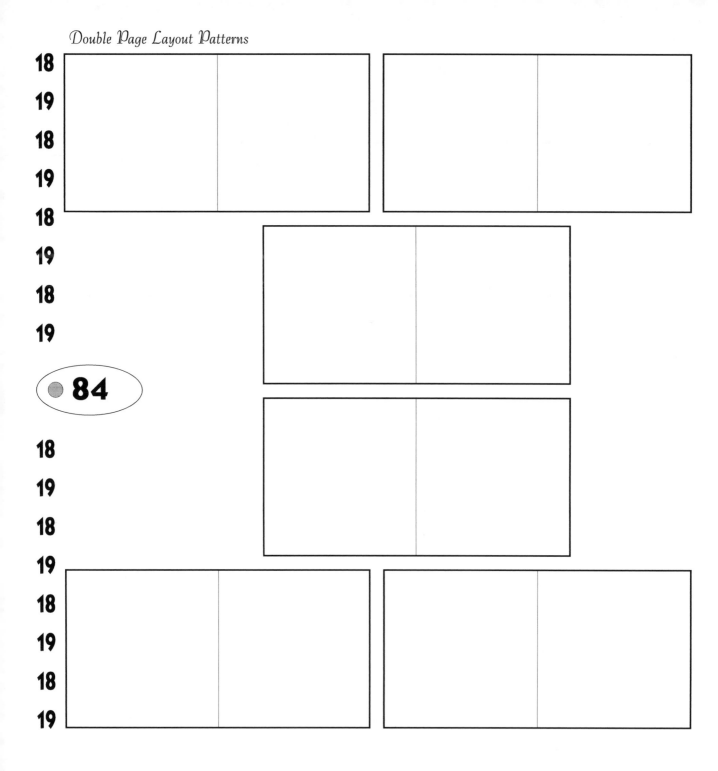

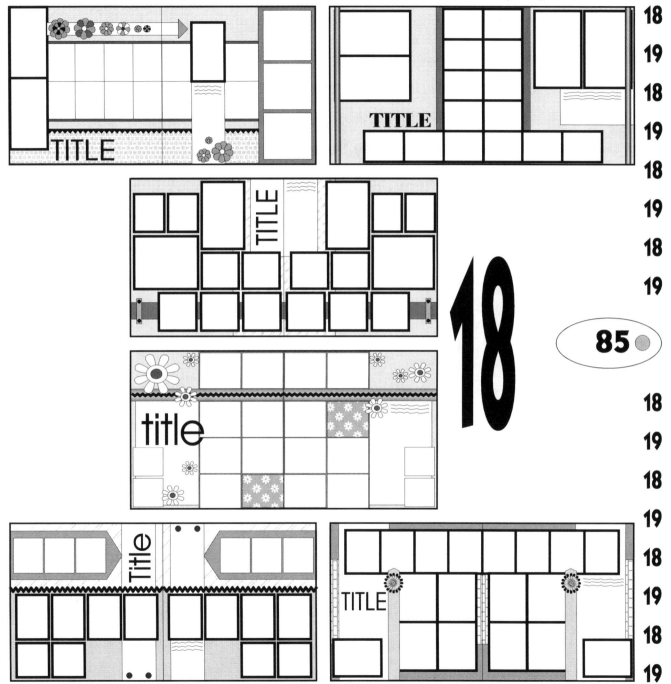

85

Double Page Layout Patterns

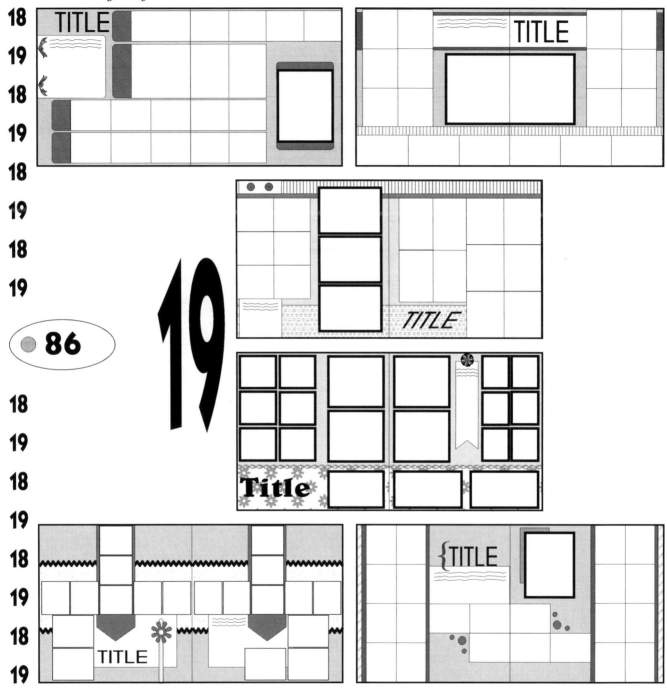

86

20
21
20
21
20
21
20
21

20
21
20
21
20
21

Double Page Layout Patterns

20
21
20
21
20
21
20
21

●**88**

20
21
20
21
20
21
20
21

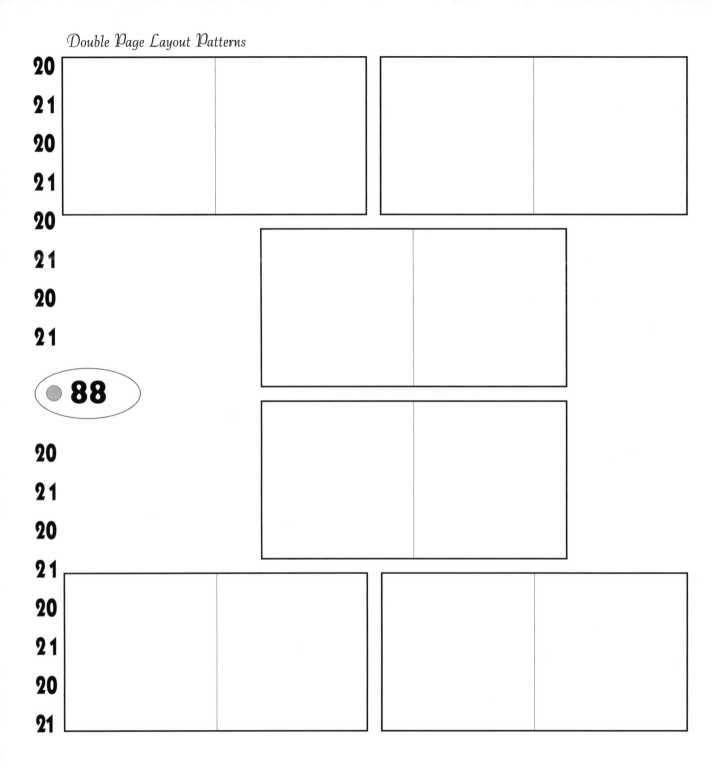

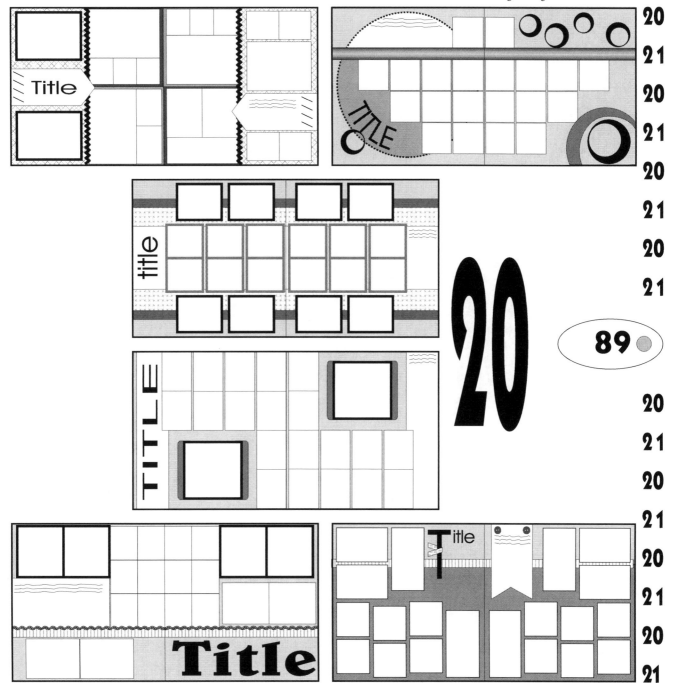

Title

TITLE

title

TITLE

20

89

Title

Title

Double Page Layout Patterns

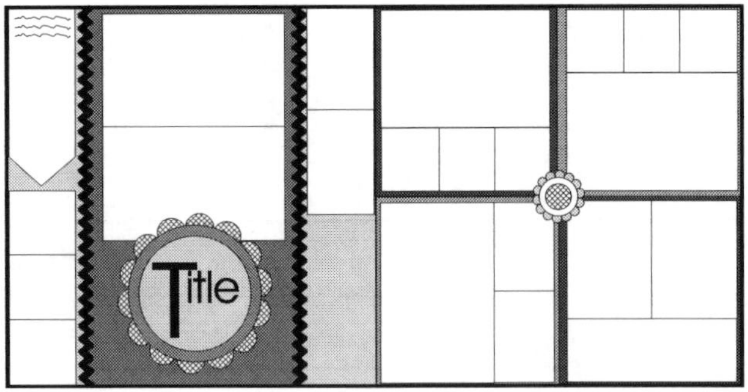

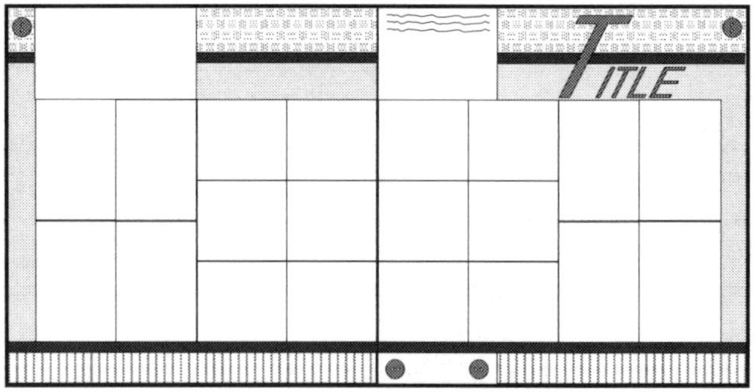

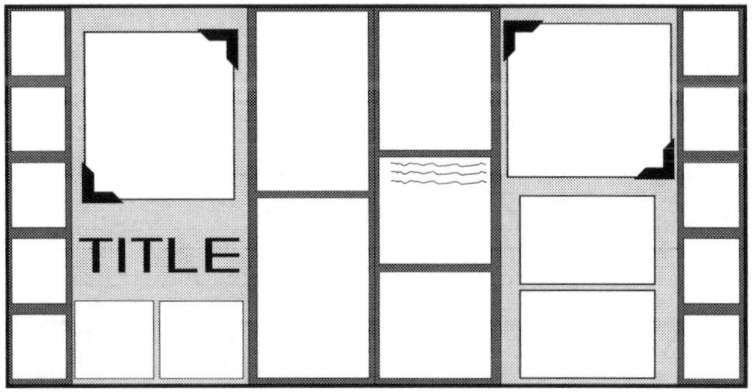

90

21

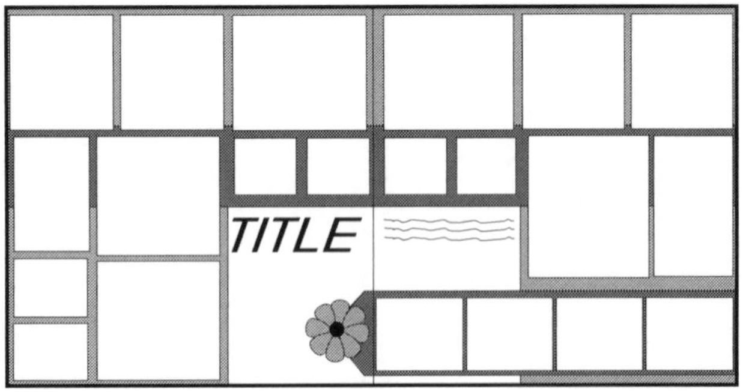

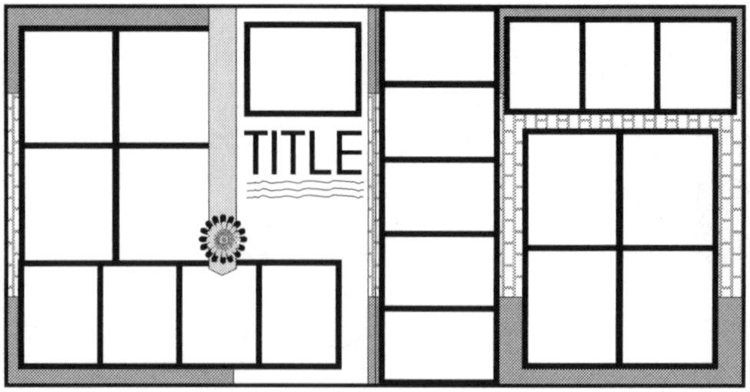

22 & 23

91

PHOTO LAYOUT PATTERNS

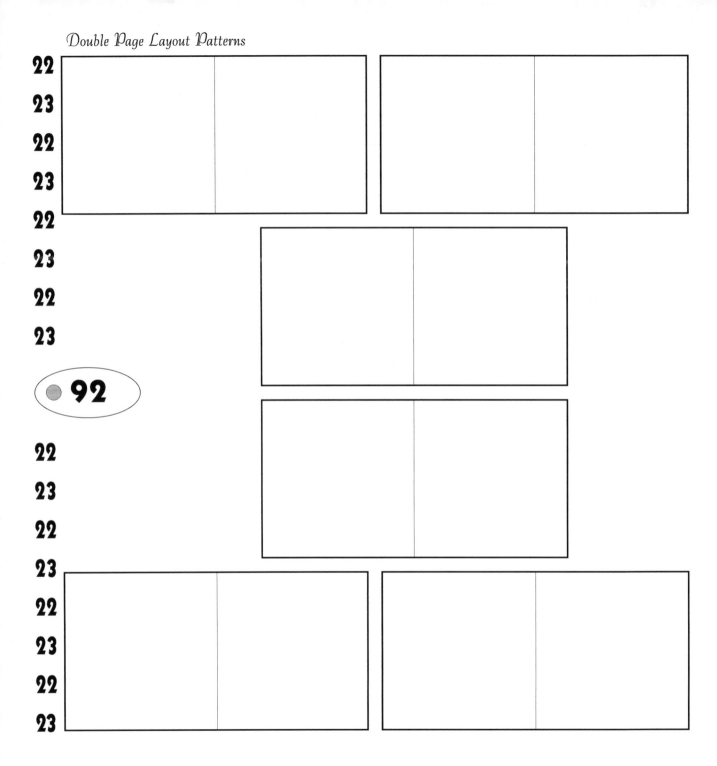

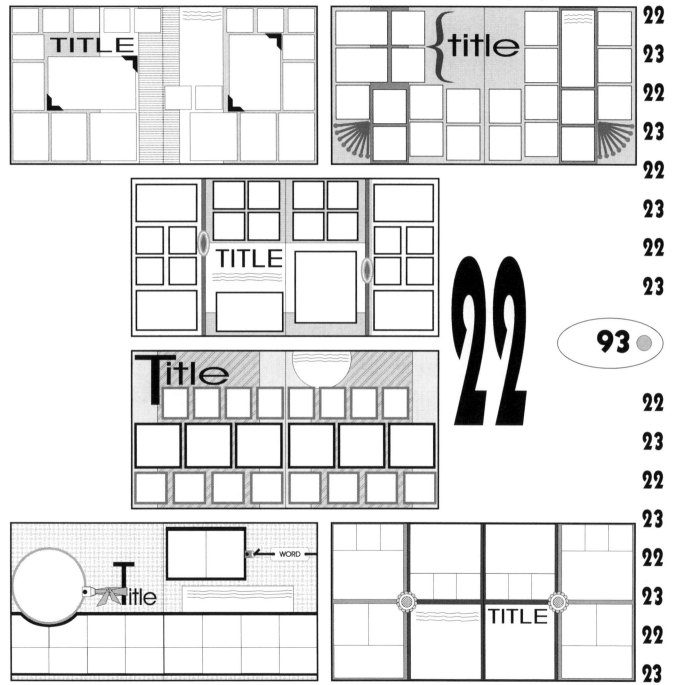

TITLE

{title

TITLE

Title

22

93

Title

WORD

TITLE

22
23
22
23
22

23
22
23

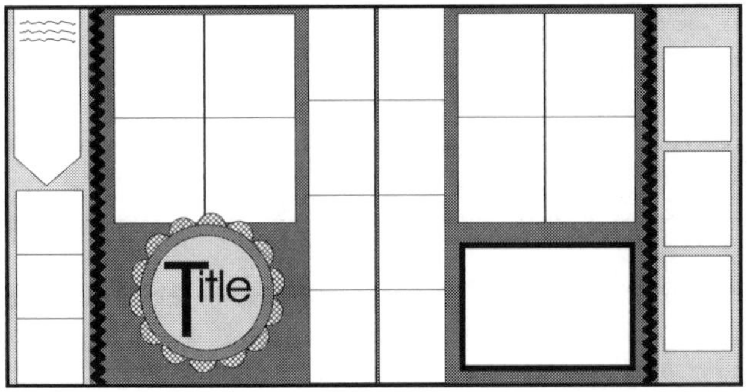

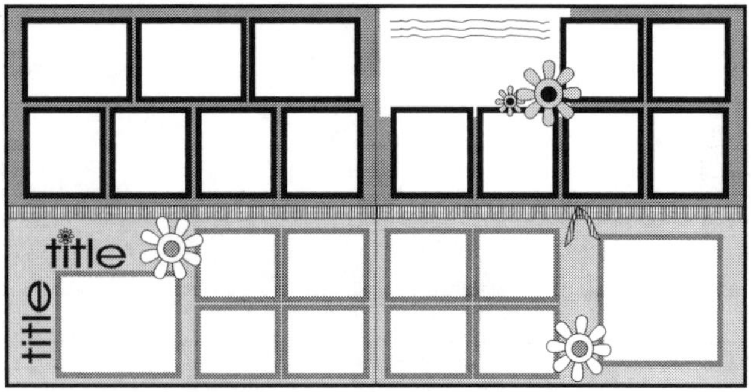

94

23

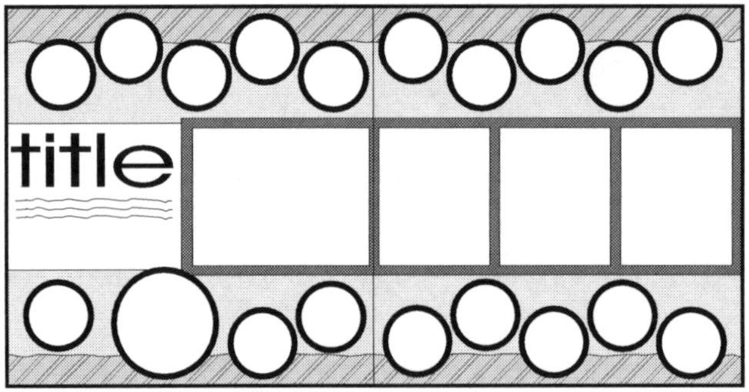

22
23
22

23
22
23
22
23

Title

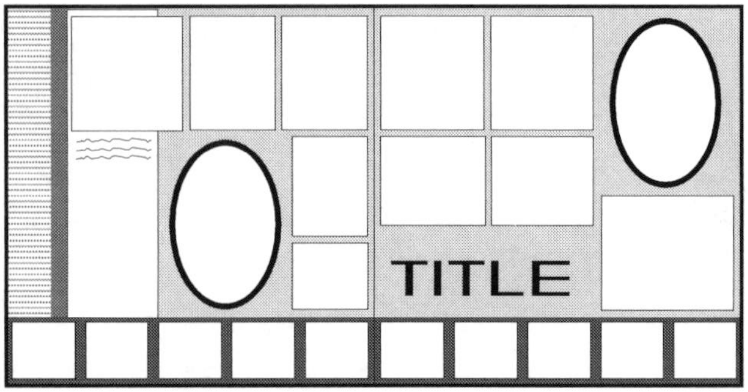

title
title
title

title

title

TITLE

TITLE

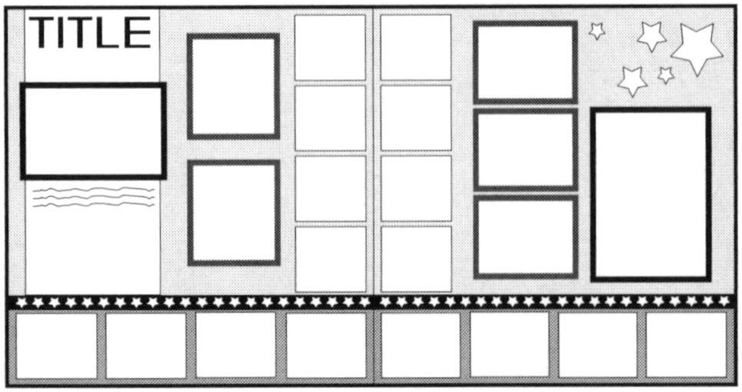

PHOTO LAYOUT PATTERNS

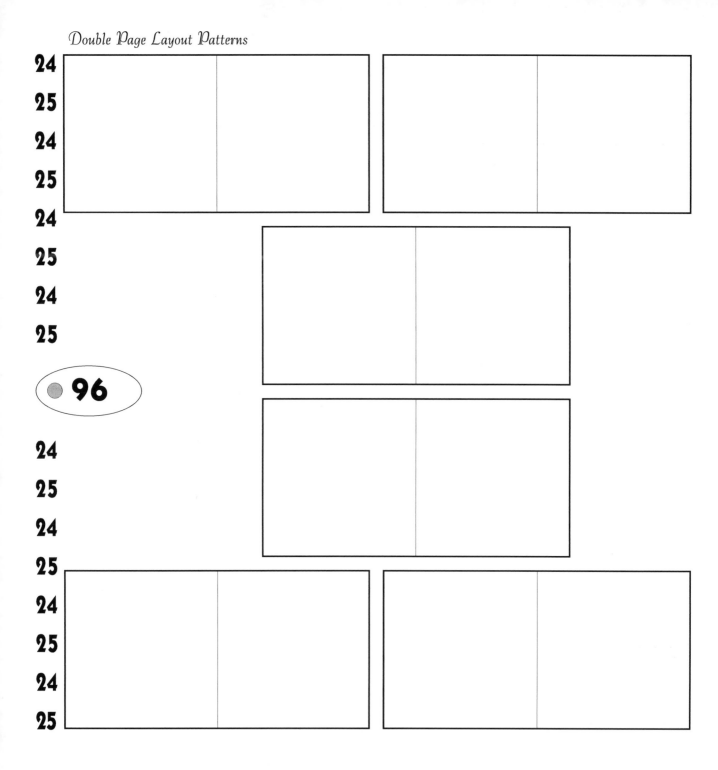

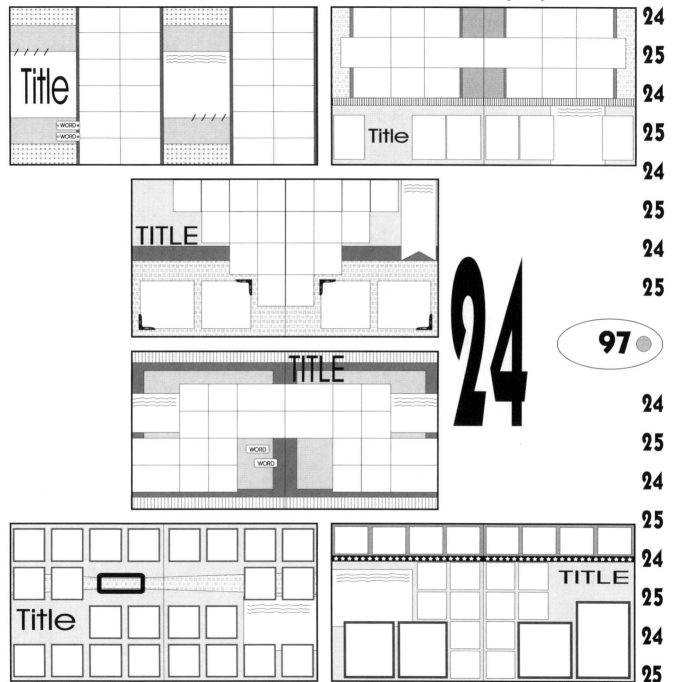

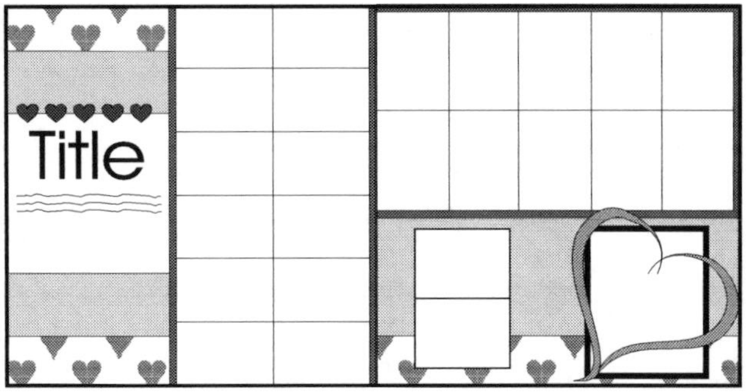

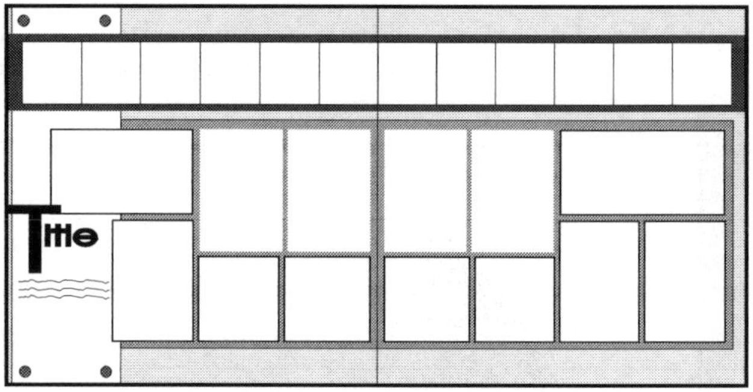

24
25
24
25
24
25
24
25

98

25

Title

Title

title

title

word

Title

TITLE

24
25
24
25
24
25

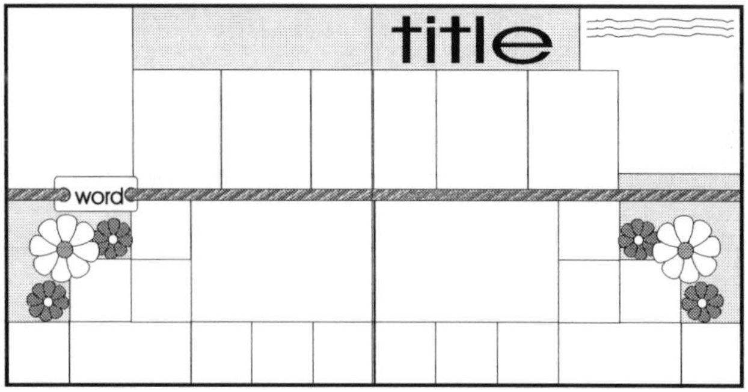

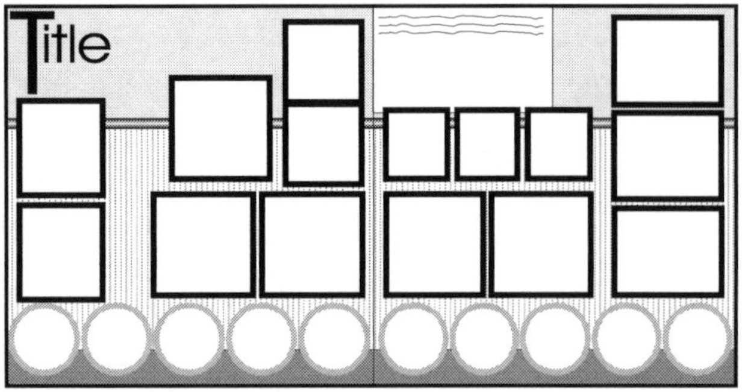

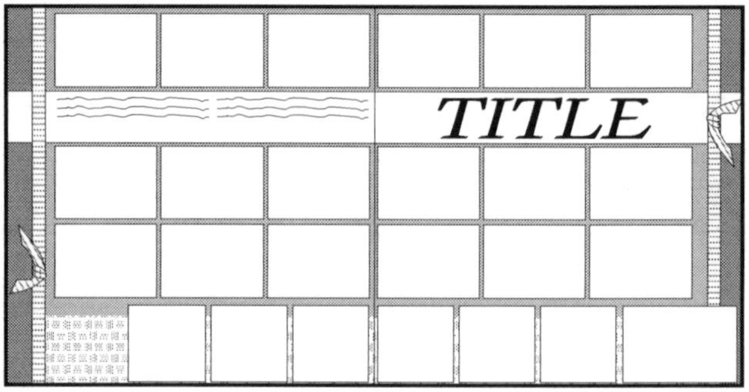

26 & 27

PHOTO LAYOUT PATTERNS

26
27
26
27
26
27
26
27

26
27
26
27
26
27
26
27

Double Page Layout Patterns

26
27
26
27
26
27
26
27

26
27
26
27
26
27
26
27

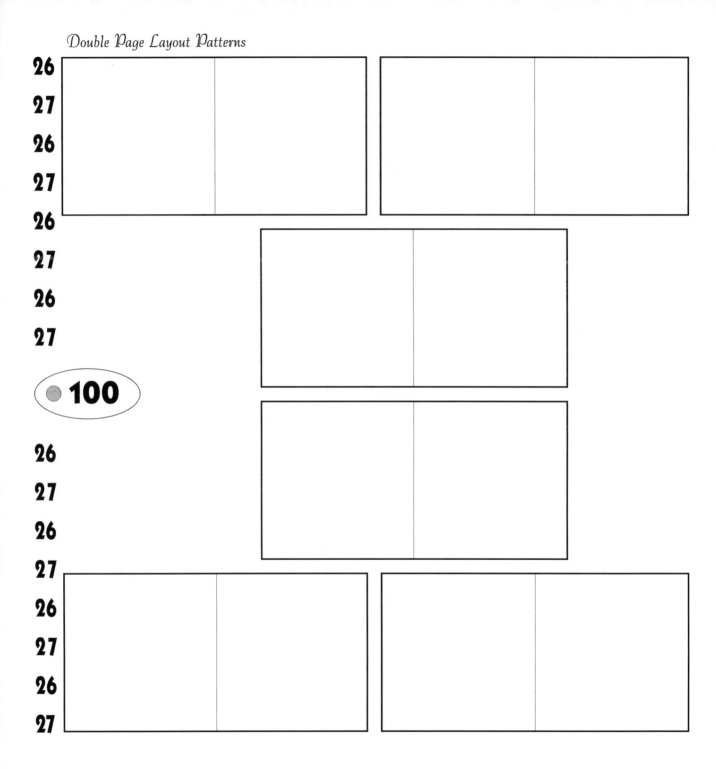

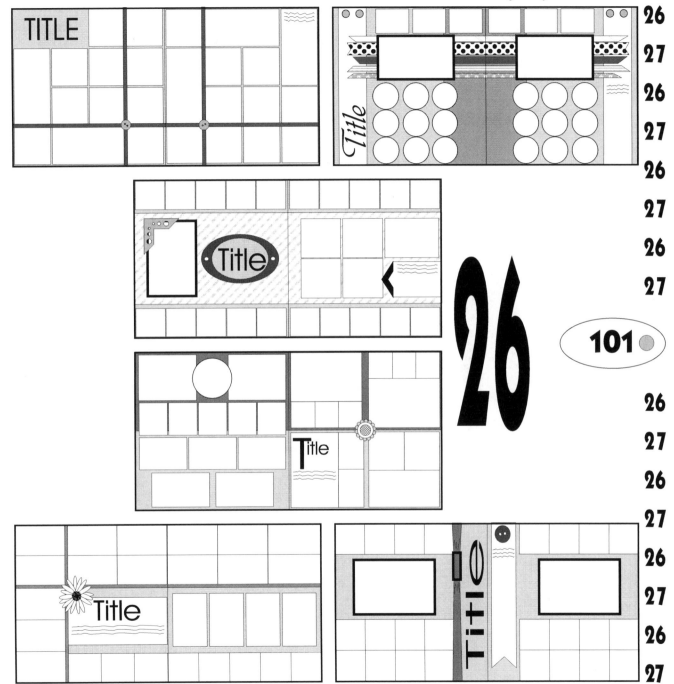

TITLE

Title

Title

Title

Title

Title

26
27
26
27
26
27
26
27

26

101

26
27
26
27
26
27

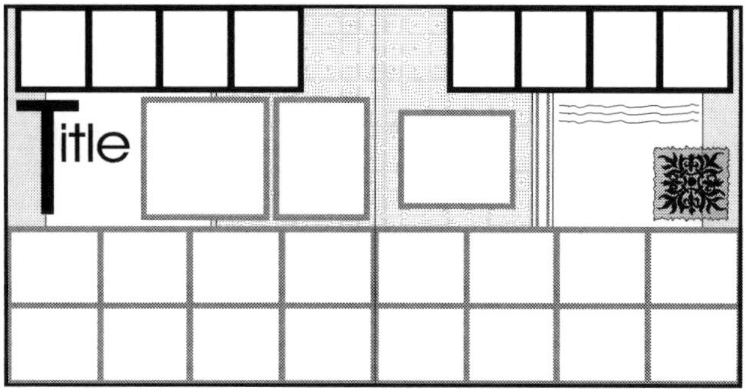

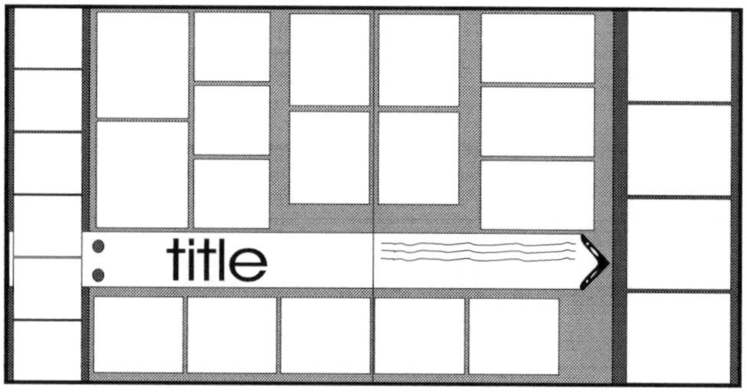

26 27 26 27 26 27 26 27

27

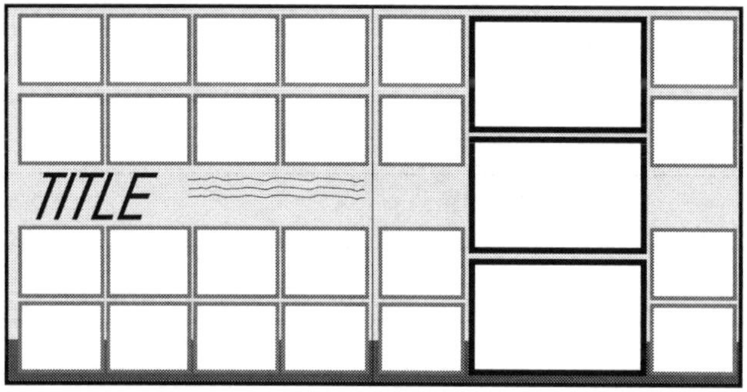

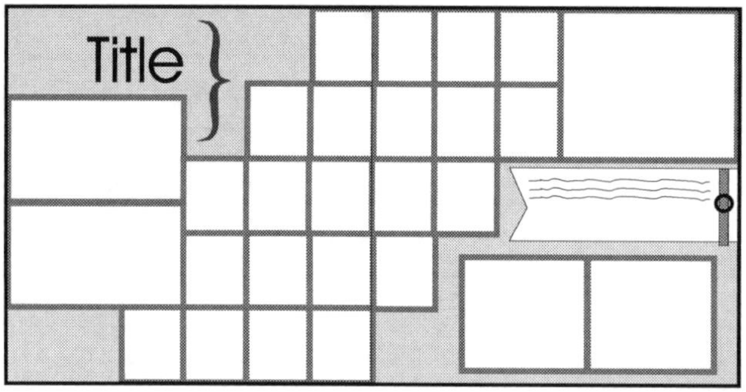

26 27 26 27 26 27 26 27

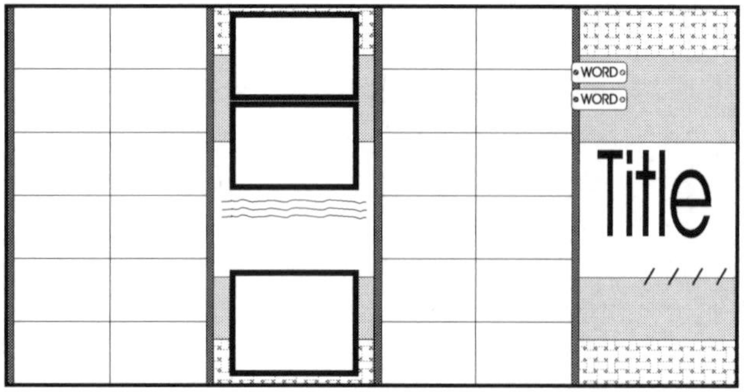

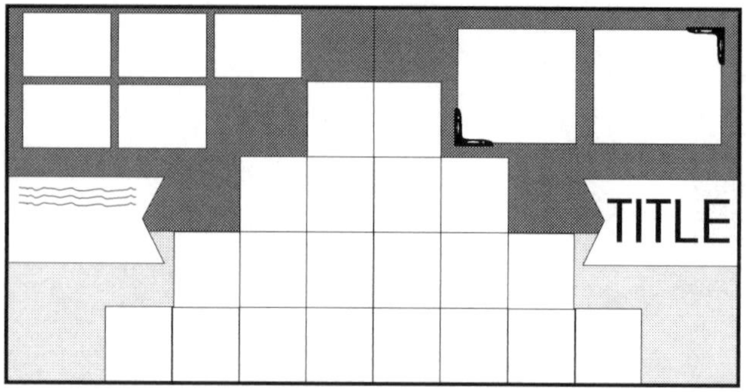

28-30

PHOTO LAYOUT PATTERNS

103

28
29
30
28
29
30
28
29

30
28
29
30
28
29
30
28

28

29

30

28

29

30

28

29

30

28

29

30

28

29

30

28

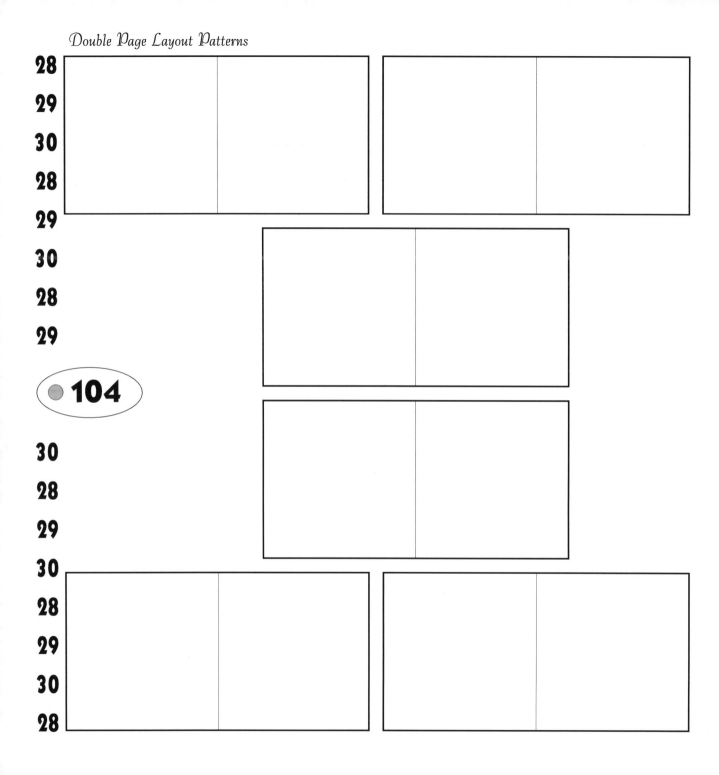

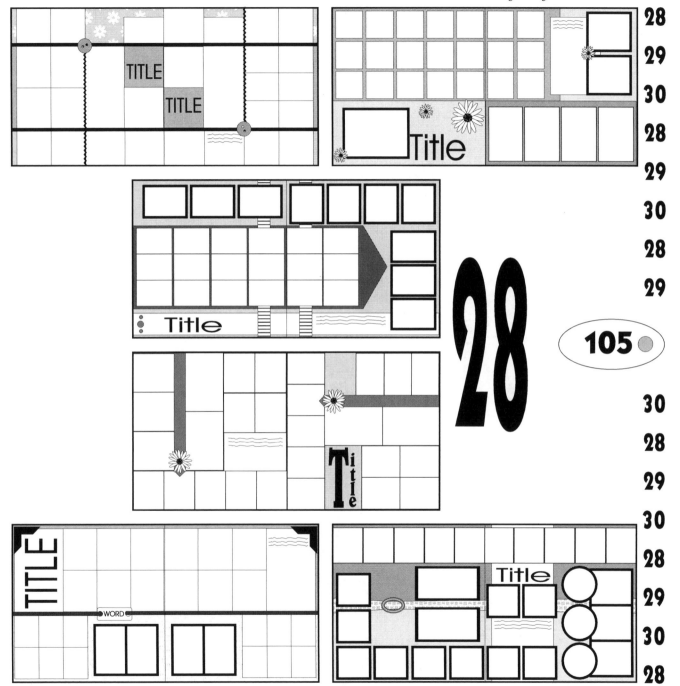

Double Page Layout Patterns

28
29
30
28
29

30
28
29

● 106

29

30
28
29
30
28
29
30
28

Title

TITLE

Title

TITLE

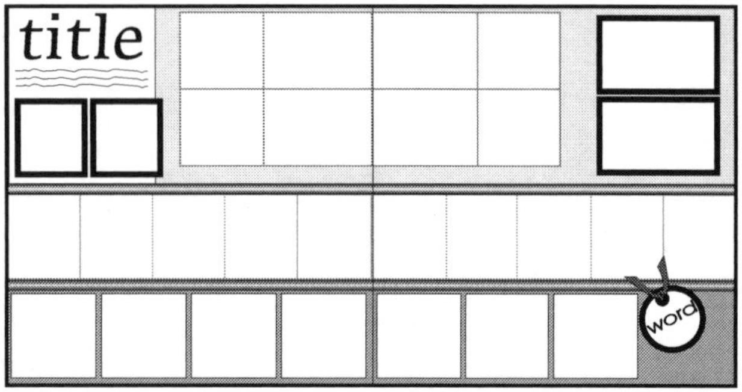

title

word

Title

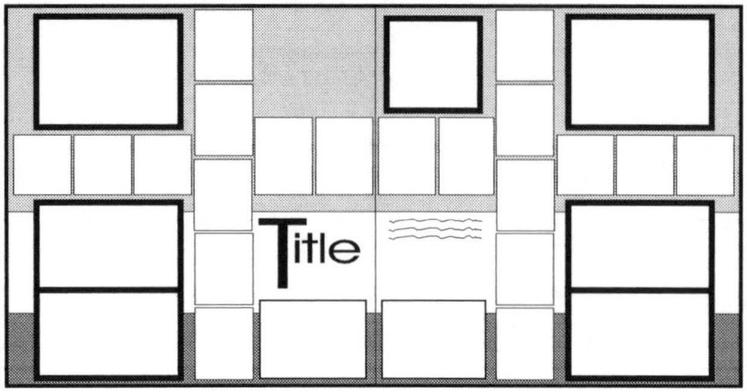

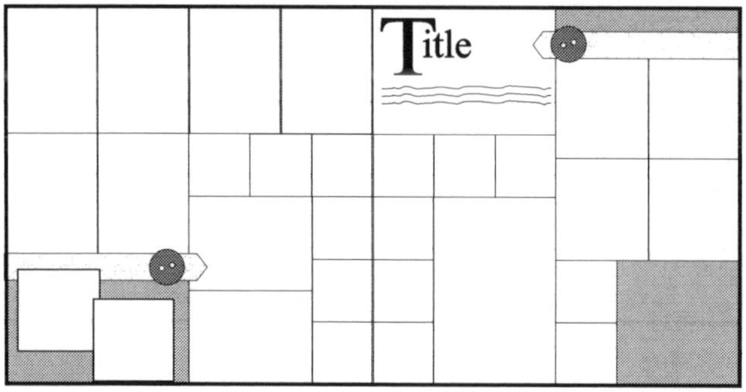

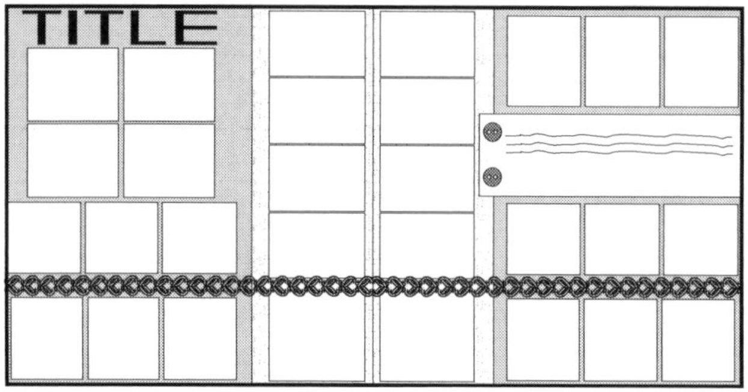

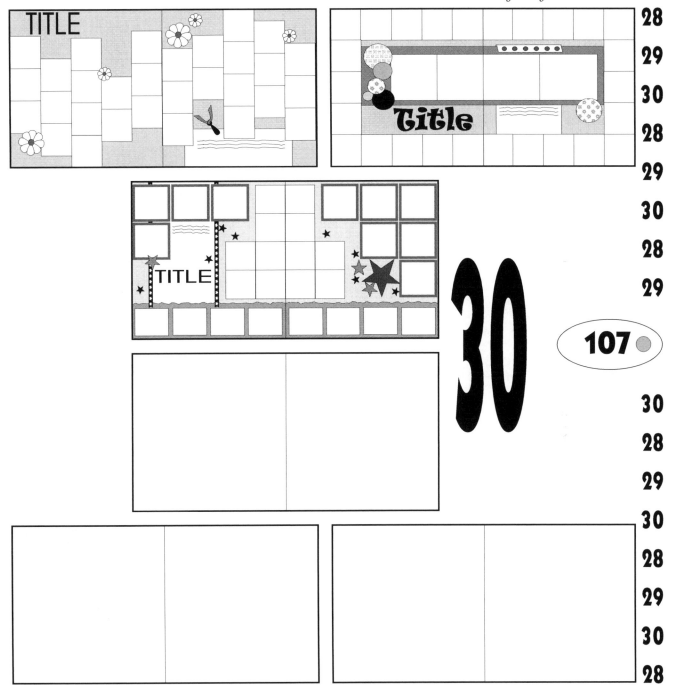

107

108

PHOTO LAYOUT PATTERNS

Single Page Layout Patterns

109

PHOTO LAYOUT PATTERNS

111

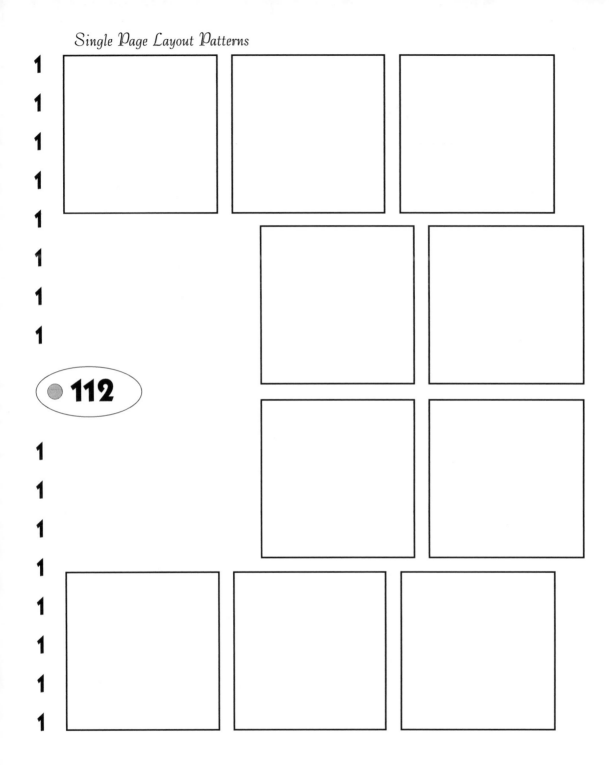

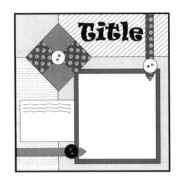

1

1

1

1

1

1

1

1

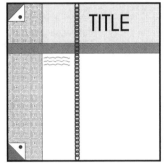

113

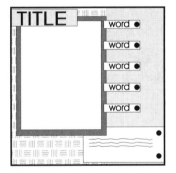

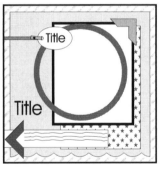

1

1

1

1

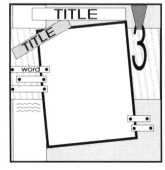

1

1

1

1

11

1
1
1
1
1
1
1
1

114

1

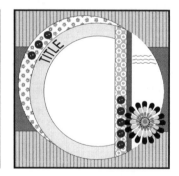

1
1
1

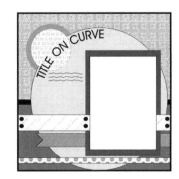
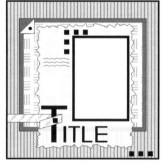

1
1
1

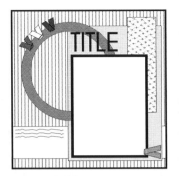

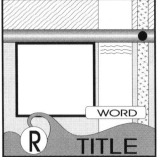

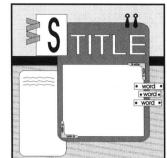

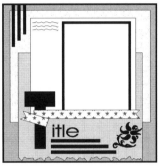

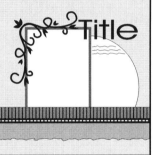

115

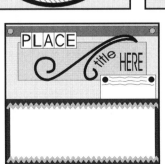

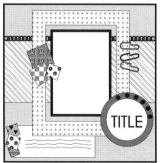

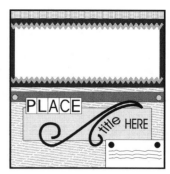

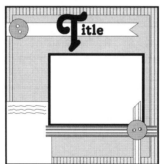

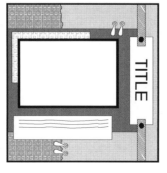
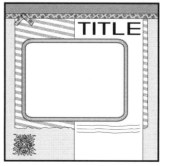

118

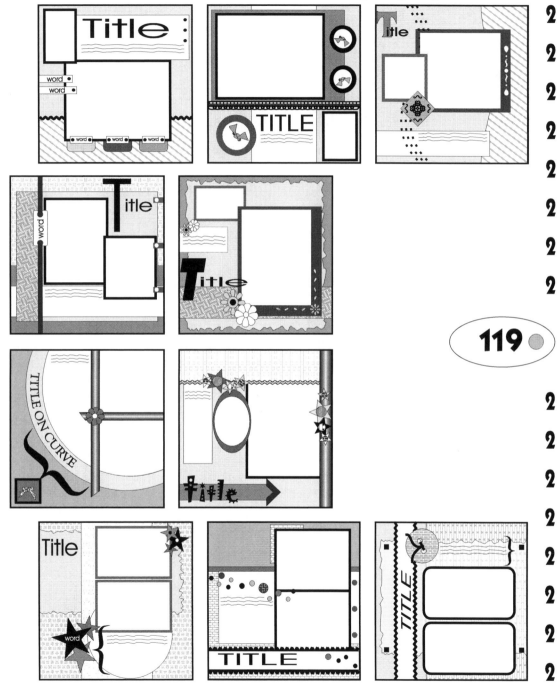

119

2
2
2
2
2
2
2
2

2
2
2
2
2
2
2

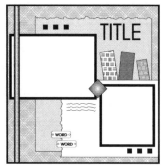
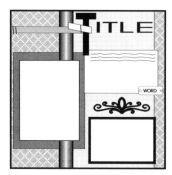

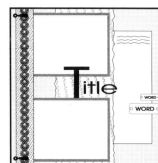
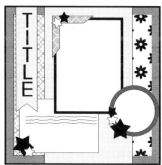

120

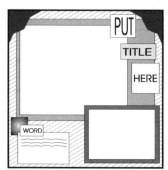

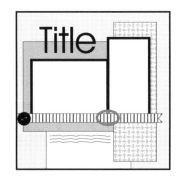

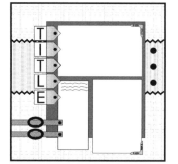

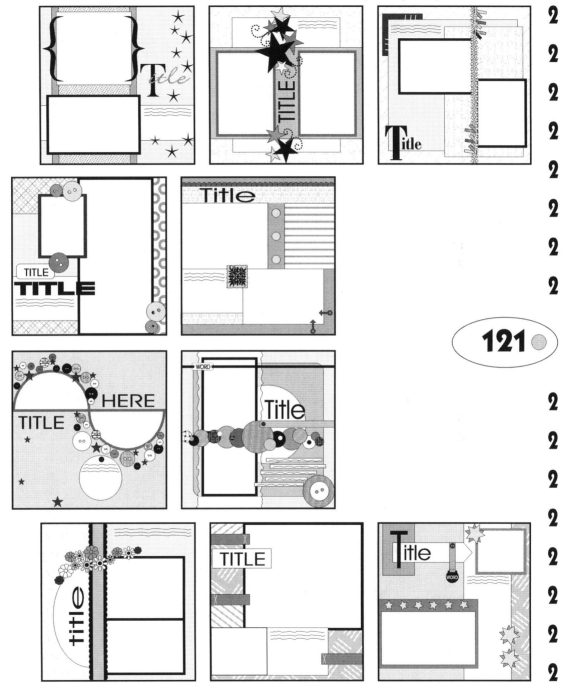

121

2
2
2
2
2
2
2
2

2
2
2
2
2
2
2

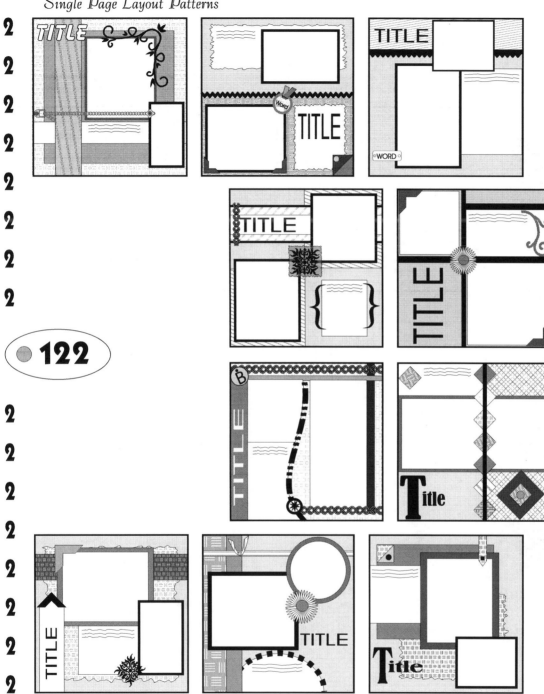

PHOTO LAYOUT PATTERNS

3

123

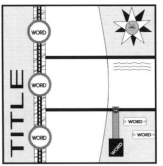

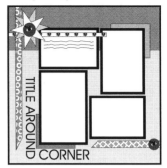

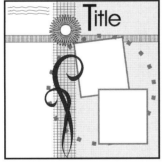

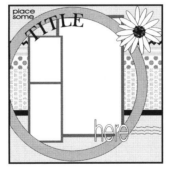

125

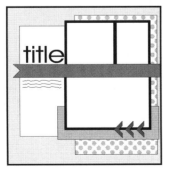

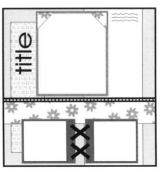

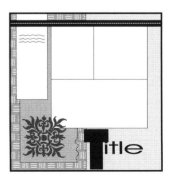

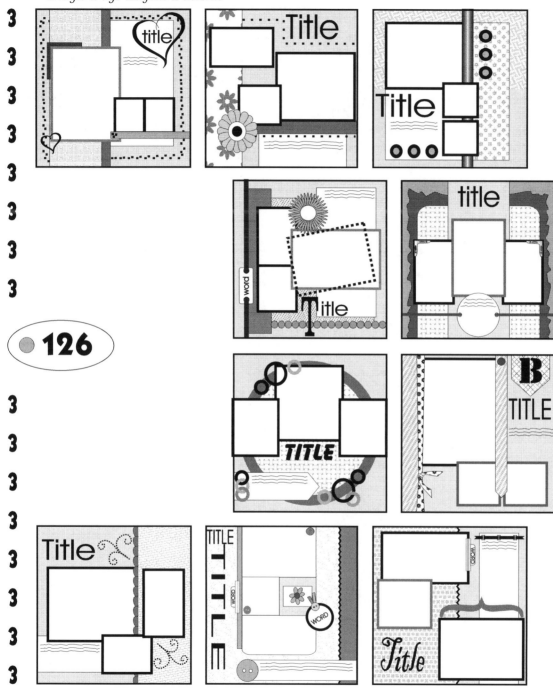

126

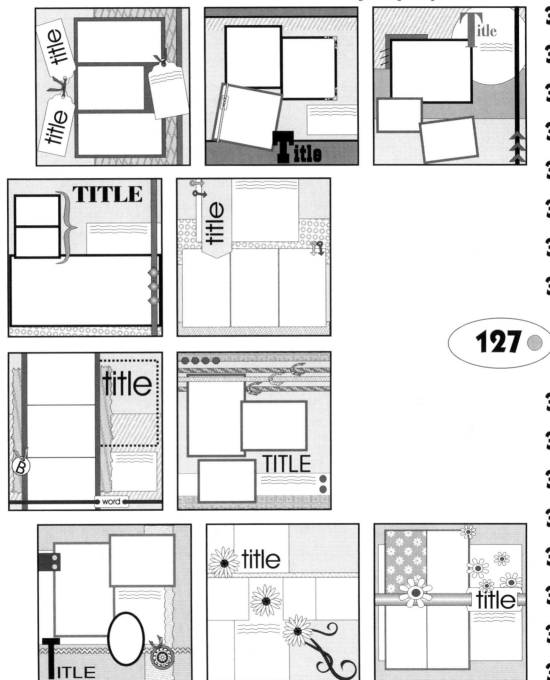

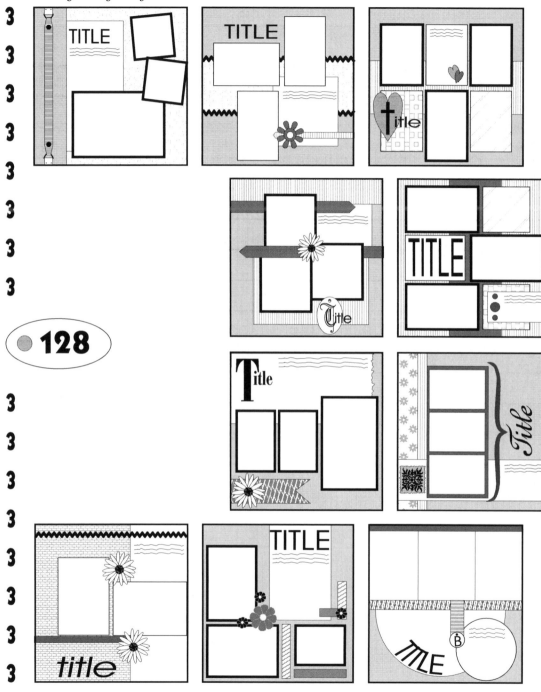

128

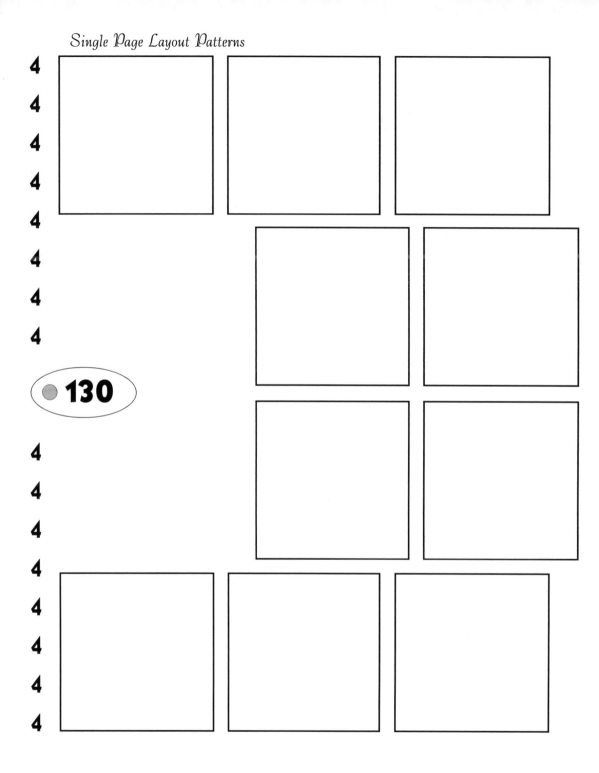

131

Single Page Layout Patterns

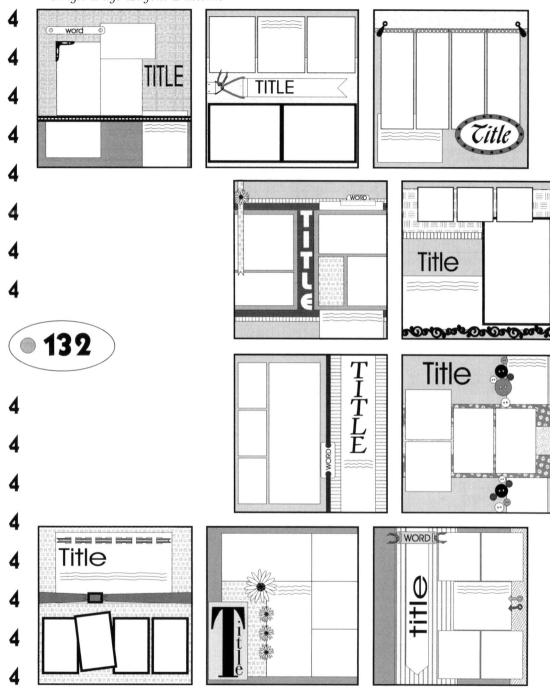

132

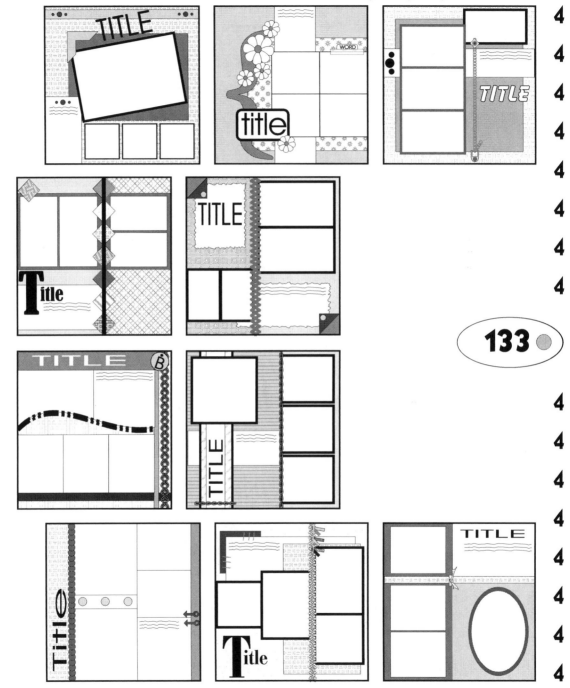

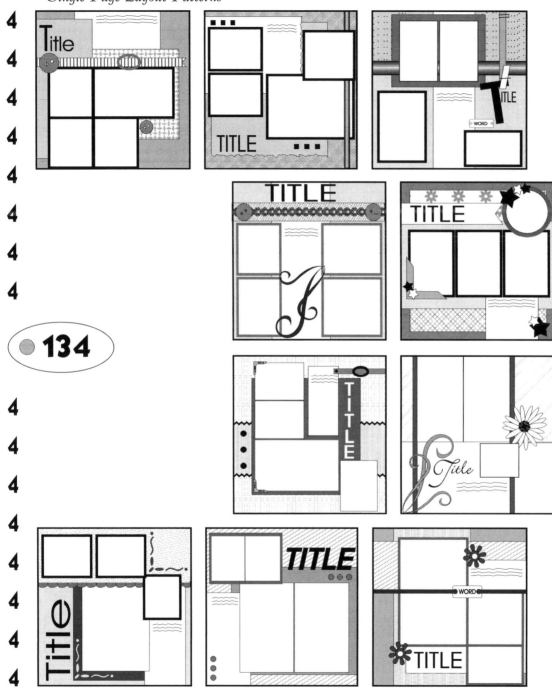

134

Photo Layout Patterns

5

135

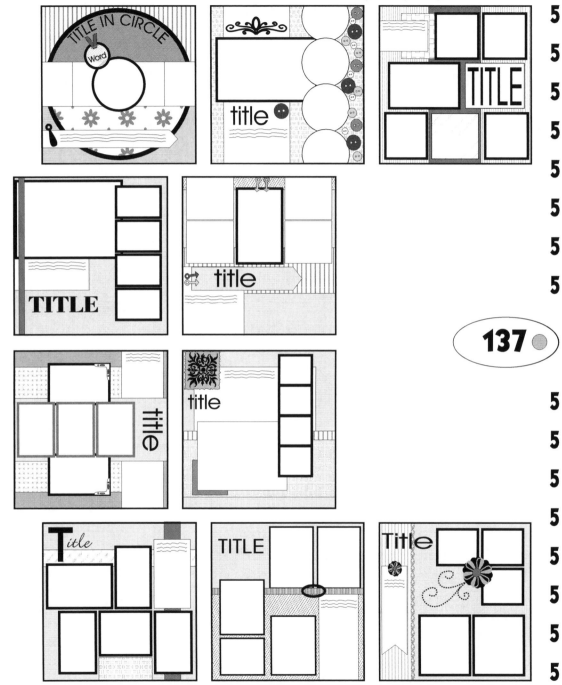

Single Page Layout Patterns

138

5
5
5
5
5

5
5
5

140

5
5
5
5
5
5
5
5

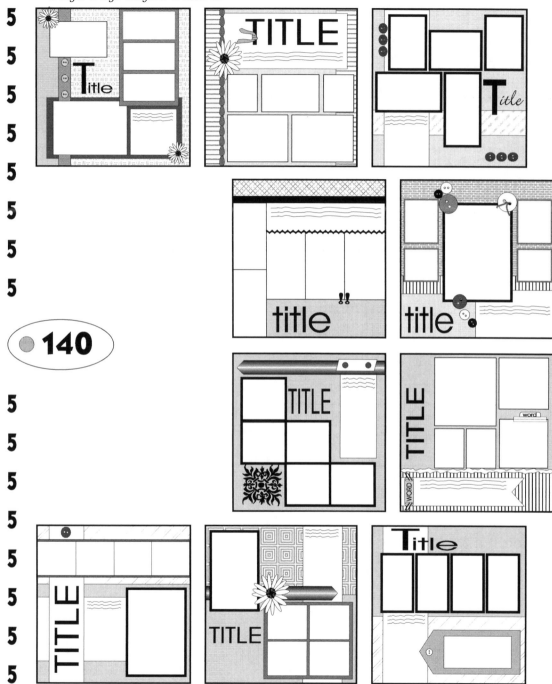

PHOTO LAYOUT PATTERNS

6
6
6
6
6
6
6
6
6
6
6
6
6
6
6
6
6
6
6
6

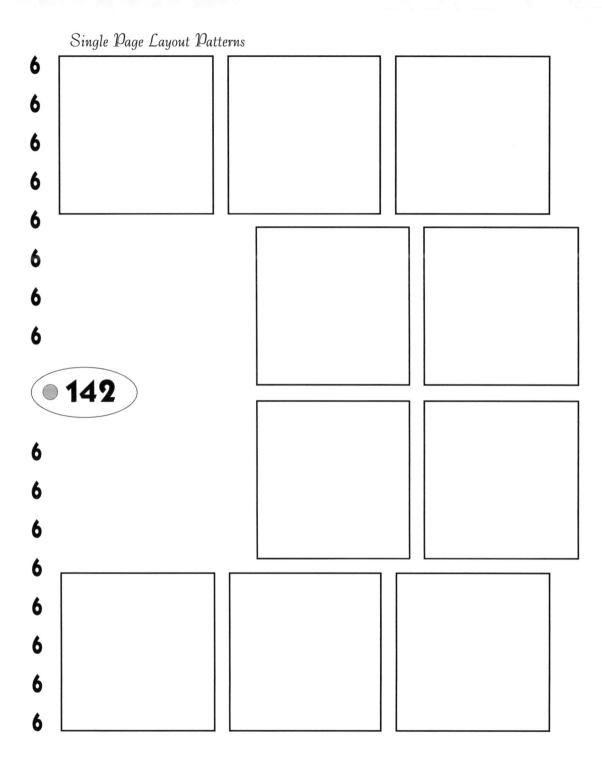

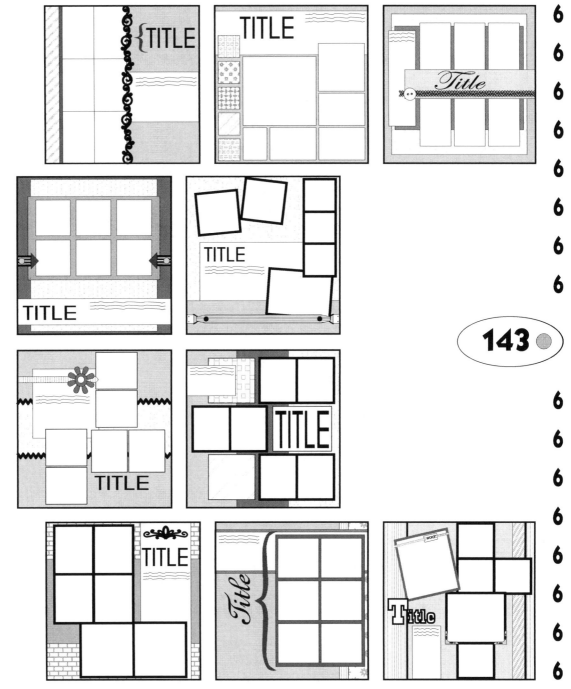

143

6
6
6
6
6
6
6
6

6
6
6
6
6
6
6
6
6
6

PHOTO LAYOUT PATTERNS

7

145

148

Photo Layout Patterns

8 & 9

149

8
9
8
9
8
9
8
9

150

8
9
8
9
8
9
8
9

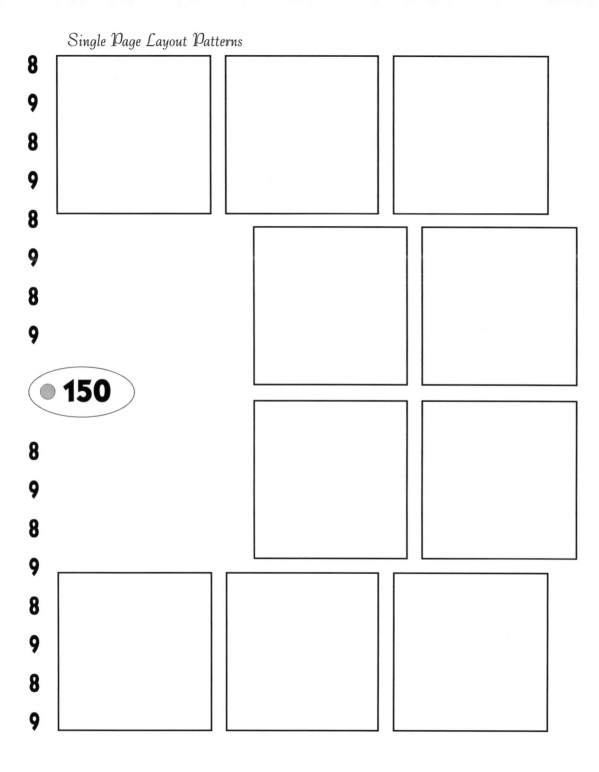

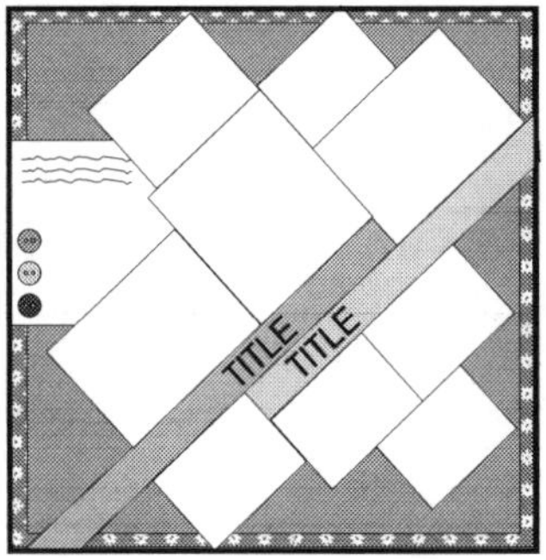
TITLE
TITLE

Title

TITLE

Title

TITLE

{TITLE

TITLE

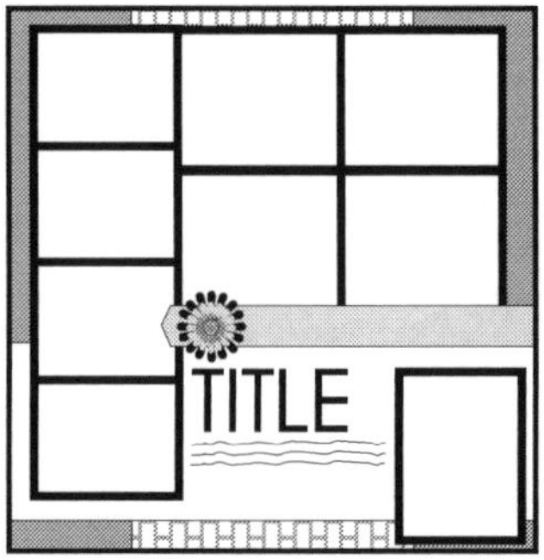
TITLE

Title

title

153

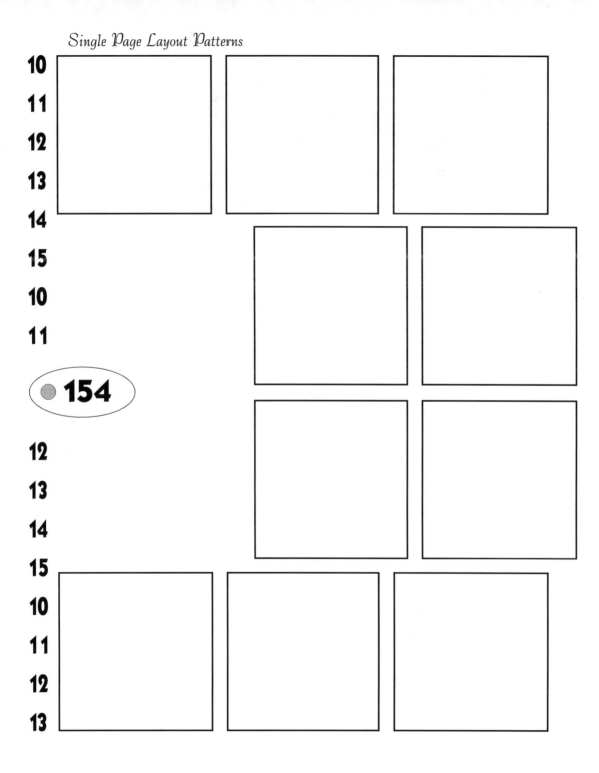

Single Page Layout Patterns

10
11
12
13
14
15
10
11

● 154

12
13
14
15
10
11
12
13

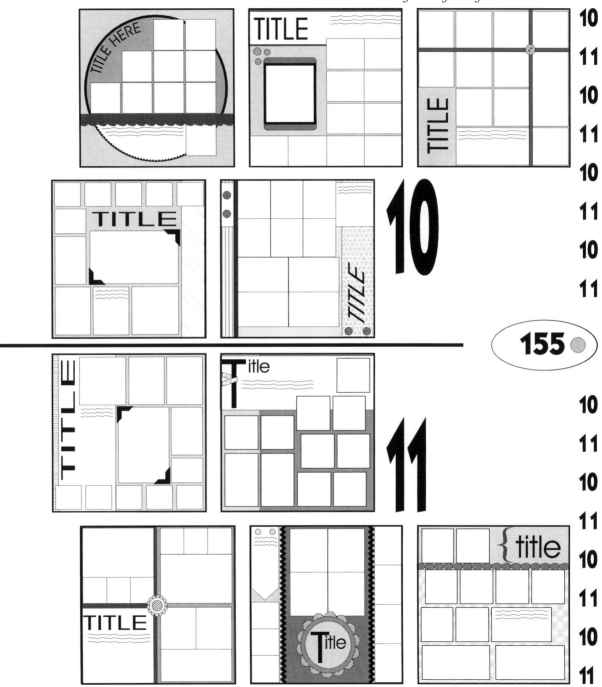

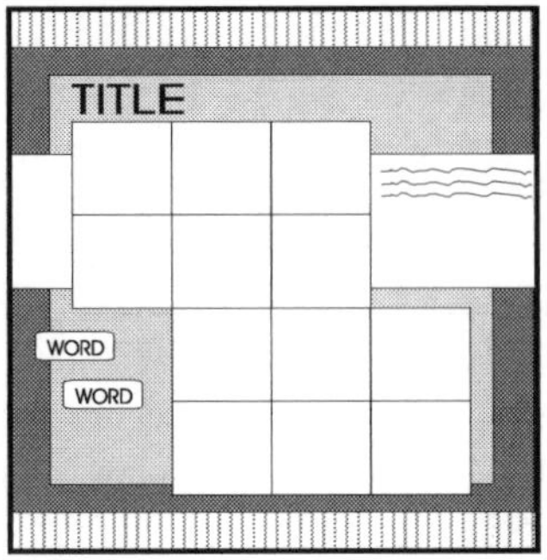

12

13

12

13

12

13

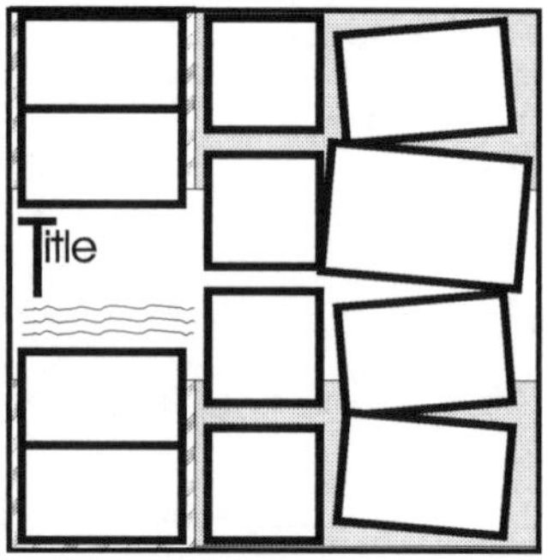

12

13

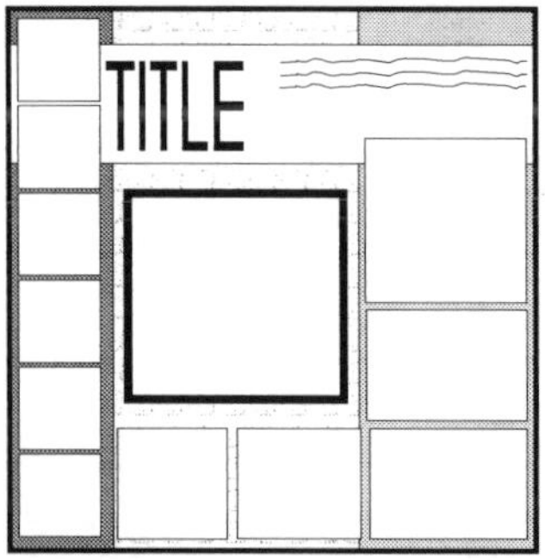

12

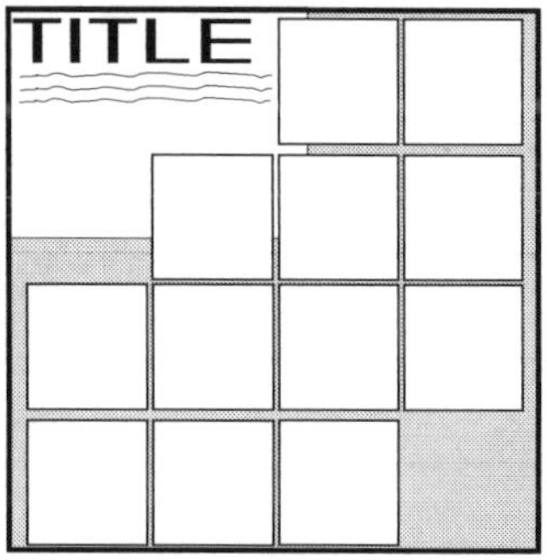

13

12

13

12

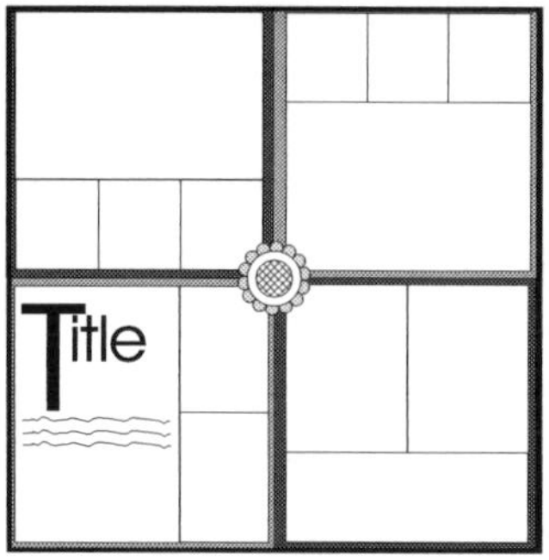

13

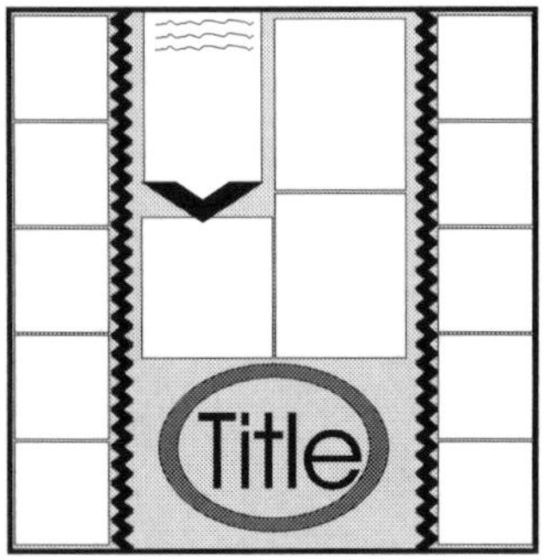

12

13

12

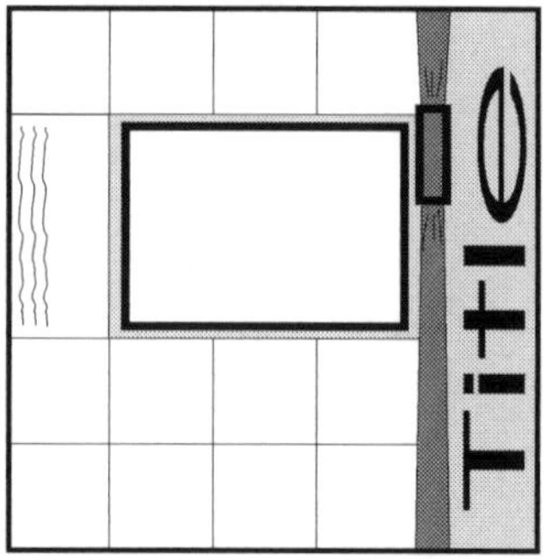

13

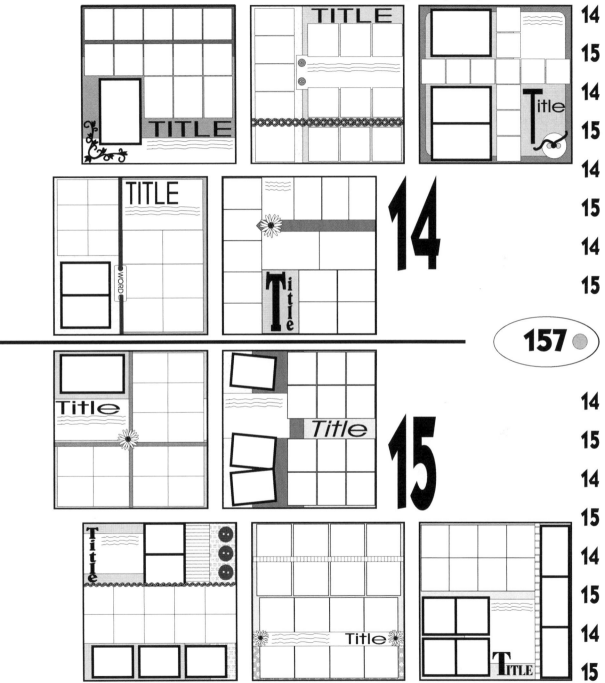

14
15
14
15
14
15
14
15

157

14
15
14
15

14
15
14
15

Patterns Size Conversion Charts

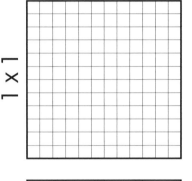

1 x 1

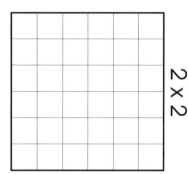

2 x 2

3 x 3

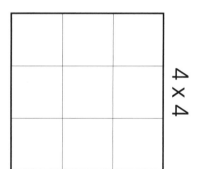

4 x 4

159

Use these conversion charts in helping to size your photos to fit the pattern your using. When fully sized, these charts and single Page Patterns are 12 x 12 and double Page Patterns are 12 x 24. Easily get correct measurements for your photos or mattings by matching your selected pattern against the conversion chart sizes.

Copy this page on to a Transparency for easier use with the Page Patterns.

Made in the
USA
Monee, IL

13987980R10090